To the women who have touched my life,

especially my daughters, Lisa and Katharine,

and most of all my wife, Elizabeth

CONTENTS

PART I
HOW TO MAKE YOUR PERSONAL FINANCIAL PLAN

Contents

PART II
HOW TO HANDLE YOUR PROPERTY

PART III

HOW YOU CAN HELP YOUR FAMILY (AND OTHERS) WHILE YOU LIVE

PART IV

HOW TO DISPOSE OF YOUR PROPERTY UPON YOUR DEATH

Contents

PART V
HOW TO SAVE TAXES YOURSELF

PART VI
HOW TO SAVE TAXES FOR YOUR FAMILY

PART VII
HOW TO GET THE PROFESSIONAL HELP
YOU NEED FOR YOUR PLAN

Contents

ACKNOWLEDGMENTS

THE FOLLOWING LAWYERS and other professionals read the manuscript, or portions of it, and made many valuable suggestions:

Edwin S. Baldwin, of Armstrong, Teasdale, Kramer & Vaughan, St. Louis, Mo.

David F. Eisner, of Fried, Frank, Harris, Shriver & Jacobson, New York

Robert L. Freedman, of Dechert Price & Rhoads, Philadelphia

Kathryn G. Henkel, of Hughes and Hill, Dallas, Texas

Ruth Ann Jones, of the University of Missouri, Columbia, Mo.

Professor William M. Jones, of the University of Missouri, Columbia, Mo.

George P. Mair, of Bingham, Dana & Gould, Boston

Lee A. Pickard, of Pickard and Gerry, Washington, D.C.

Lawrence B. Rodman, of Rodman & Rodman, New York

Karen A. Vagts, of Cambridge, Mass.

Dean Bruce Wolk, of the University of California at Davis, School of Law.

The following people undertook to read the manuscript, or portions of it, from the standpoint of the women for whom the book was written. Their comments were particularly helpful in rooting out legal jargon and in anticipating questions readers might ask:

Carol Ackerman	Ruth Kuhn
Jerry Ackerman	Ulla Malkus
Anne Büchi	Marion McGilvray
George H. Büchi	Ellen W. Mering
Susan E. Davis	Barbara L. Oldman
Esther Fenerjian	Dorothy K. Reuss
Elizabeth L. Fletcher	Robert L. Reuss
Caroline E. E. Hartwig	Carol Roehm
Elinor Horan	Florence W. Trullinger
Anne H. Howe	Stephen K. Urice
Walter S. Kerr, Jr.	John P. Willson
Frank Kuhn	Linda Willson

My research assistants, all members of the Harvard Law School Class of 1984, made valuable contributions in many ways:

Frances M. Horner	Gary M. Reiff
Carla Muñoz	

The careful, painstaking work of the publisher's editorial staff was a major help in making the manuscript clearer and more readable.

Grateful acknowledgment is given to the publishers of my other books for permission to adapt portions from:

Estate Planning Cases and Text, by David Westfall, Copyright © 1982, Foundation Press, Inc.

Estate Planning Law and Taxation, by David Westfall,

My secretary, Lori A. Williams, did her usual fine work in typing and assembling the manuscript. Deborah R. Gallagher and other members of the word-processing staff of the Harvard Law School were patient, persevering, and indispensable in helping me polish the final product.

Finally, my mother-in-law, Dorothy S. Beatty, and my wife, Elizabeth B. Westfall, were both inspirations for the book and important sources of encouragement, suggestions, and support.

EVERY WOMAN'S
GUIDE TO
FINANCIAL PLANNING

How This Book Can Help You

THIS BOOK is for every woman who wants to know more about making her money work harder for her and her family. Important as this information is, it is not always easy to find. During my twenty-nine years at the Harvard Law School, I have taught estate planning to thousands of students. Your lawyer may have been one of them. These highly qualified young men and women are a truly exceptional group. Yet few of them begin my course with the knowledge they need in order to make their own financial choices wisely. If you were in my class, you might ask the same questions they have asked me over the years—questions that are answered in this book.

Although both men and women need this information about financial planning, it is particularly important for women, as they are more likely than men to have responsibility for managing money suddenly thrust on them. This can happen as a result of divorce or upon the death of a parent or husband, or simply as a result of a woman's decision to become financially independent. To consider just one of these factors, the odds are two-to-one that a husband will die first, often leaving his widow with new and unfamiliar tasks.

My mother-in-law was in that situation after her husband died eight years ago. She had handled her own investments successfully for years. But after her husband's death she had two entirely new roles to play—as executor in settling his estate and carrying out the terms of his will, and as trustee of a trust he had created. She also wanted to revise her own financial plan as the family situation changed over the years.

This book is the result of many talks we had about these matters. I realized that if these new responsibilities were bewildering to my mother-in-law, they must be even more so to other women who do not have her experience in dealing with investments. And, of course, few women have a lawyer to turn to, as she does, who will answer their questions without charging a fee. What would I tell other women if I could talk to each one individually? What financial information will my wife need if I die before she does? What will I tell my own daughters (and sons as well) when they are old enough to be interested in financial planning?

4

I discovered that there was no book that would give my mother-in-law the information she needed in clear, nonlegal language. Some books would have compelled her to wade through a mass of details to find the specific items she was interested in. Others were too narrow and specialized, concentrating on a single aspect of financial planning, such as saving taxes, and ignoring the rest. I decided to write this book to tell women like her what they need to know about all of the major aspects of financial planning. This book is intended to be both comprehensive and jargon free.

No book—not even this one—is a substitute for a lawyer. If you read this book *before* you meet with your lawyer and refer to it again to answer your questions *after* your meeting, you will know more about your financial plan and your choices in carrying it out. You and your lawyer will be able to work much better together.

This book can help you save time for your lawyer. If you are familiar with what is in it, your lawyer will find out more quickly what you want to do with your money and will need less time to explain different ways you can handle it. If you save your lawyer's time, you will be saving your money. If the charge is $75 an hour—and some city lawyers charge twice that much—you will have paid for this book several times over if it helps you save even one hour of time!

My hope, then, is that you will find in this book the information you need in order to make and carry out a personal financial plan with a lawyer's help. To make your money do the most for you and your family, you will need to know how to:

1. Make your own financial plan
2. Use your money for yourself
3. Help your family while you live
4. Bequeath your property
5. Save taxes
6. Help your family save taxes
7. Get professionals to help you

Each part of this book deals with one of these topics.

Please read all of part 1 first because it is the key to the entire book. It tells how you can make your plan and where you can find what you will need in the other parts of the book.

To make your own financial plan, you need to know what you have, what you want to do with it, how the tools of estate planning can help you, and what problems to avoid in using these tools. Only you can decide what you want to do with your money, so part 1 deals with the other three aspects of making your financial plan.

In chapter 1, you will learn how to figure out what you have, including property you don't actually own but can dispose of. You may be surprised to find how much you have to work with, especially when you add in such items as benefits provided by your employer which are payable upon your retirement or death.

Chapter 2 introduces you to the basic tools of estate planning—including gifts, trusts, wills, and joint ownership—and shows you how to use them.

Chapter 3 describes and shows you how to avoid

the three biggest roadblocks in carrying out your plan: taxes, costs, and husbands. Both chapters 2 and 3 tell you where in this book to turn for more information about particular topics.

You may want to stop right here and skip to part 1. The rest of this introduction describes how the other six parts can help you carry out your plan, once made.

Are you wondering about the best way to use your money for yourself? Part 2 shows you a number of different ways. Chapter 4 covers whose name your property should be in—your own individually, in joint names with someone else, or in the name of a trustee for you. Chapter 5 deals with how to handle your investments, including stocks, bank accounts, and mutual funds. Chapter 6 tells how you may protect your rights under someone else's financial plan. If a parent or your husband has made an arrangement for you, how can you be sure you are getting all that you have coming to you under it?

Are you concerned with helping your family and any other people you want to provide for? Again, there are many different ways, and these are discussed in part 3. Chapter 7 covers how to make a gift and what the different rules are for real estate, securities, and other property. Chapter 8 shows how to use trusts (and substitutes for trusts) to make gifts. Few people fully appreciate the possibilities that trusts offer to make their money work for themselves and their family. Every woman who is considering making a big gift should first read chapter 8 to see if she wants to make the gift through a trust. Finally, chapter 9 shows that there are many ways to help people financially other than through gifts. This is important because you may save taxes if you can avoid making a gift.

Are you concerned with how to dispose of your property when you die? Part 4 describes different ways to do this. You need a will, of course, and chapter 10 shows what a will can—and cannot—do for you. Chapter 11 is about "living" trusts—trusts that benefit you during your lifetime and then continue for your family (or others). Finally, chapter 12 shows how trusts that are set up either in your will or during your life can take care of your family.

Are you worried about saving taxes? Part 5 points the way. Chapter 13 shows how you can use the tools of estate planning to save income taxes. Chapter 14 deals with ways to save gift taxes on any gifts you make. Finally, chapter 15 deals with keeping down estate and inheritance taxes.

Are you concerned about saving taxes for your family? You should be. When you make gifts of income-producing property to your children, you may be piling up income taxes for them in the future. There also may be taxes when they pass the property on to their children. Part 6 tells how you can keep down all of these taxes. Chapter 16 describes ways to save estate and gift taxes for your children, as well as the "generation-skipping transfer tax" that came into the tax law in 1976. Chapter 17 shows how you can use the tools of estate planning to save income taxes for your children and grandchildren.

Do you want to know more about the professionals who can help you with your financial plan—when to use them and how to find them? Part 7 tells how to choose—and use effectively—lawyers, accountants, trustees, and executors. It also discusses when and why you may need to review your financial plan to bring it up to date.

Finally, the glossary at the end of the book will assist you by explaining in clear, nontechnical language the legal terms that are used in financial planning. Although such terms have been avoided here, you may encounter them elsewhere and may need to know what they mean.

PART I

HOW TO MAKE
YOUR PERSONAL
FINANCIAL PLAN

I N ORDER *to make your own financial plan, you
need to know what you have, how the tools of estate
planning can help you, and how to avoid problems in
using those tools.*

*Knowing what you have to dispose of can itself be
tricky because wealth can be held in so many different forms. For example, property may be held by you
individually, or jointly with your husband or someone
else. Property also may be held for your benefit under
an arrangement that gives you the power to dispose
of property that you do not actually own. Lawyers call
such an arrangement a "power of appointment." If
you have such a power, deciding whether or not to
use it, and in what way, is an important part of making your financial plan. Chapter 1 includes a checklist*

to help you figure out what property you either own or have some control over.

Many women who know what they can dispose of and who they want to help financially are not fully aware of the range of estate-planning tools that can be used to carry out a plan. The best-known tools are wills, but chapter 2 discusses a number of other tools, including trusts, and shows how they can be used to carry out your plan.

In addition to knowing what is yours to dispose of and how you can use the tools of estate planning, you may need to know how to deal with three potential roadblocks. Of these, taxes are the best known, but for many women two other roadblocks—the cost of making and carrying out their plans and the rights of their husbands—may be even more important in determining how effective their plans will be. Chapter 3 discusses all three of these roadblocks.

CHAPTER 1

What You Have to Work With

ALTHOUGH you probably have a good idea of what property is in your own name, you may not know how much you could sell it for if it is not a bank account or a security with prices quoted in the newspaper. In addition, you may not know what property is under your control but not in your name alone. For example, your home or your checking account may be in joint names with another person. Does this mean you have no control over it? The answer depends on state law, but often you have the right to dispose of part or all of this property if you follow the necessary legal steps.

Determining what property is yours to work with should come first, before you decide what you want to do with it. The amount involved may not be large enough to provide for anyone but you. In that case, the problem will be how to use your property to meet your own needs. If you have more than enough to cover those needs, you may also want to provide for other people or for charities.

You may also want to estimate what part of the property you own or control will be counted in figuring the federal estate tax. If you do not own or control $325,000 or more and have made no substantial gifts, your estate will not be subject to this tax.

Your lawyer can give you an estimate of your "taxable estate" on which the federal estate tax is figured. Generally, it includes everything you own and any insurance on your life if you can name the beneficiary. (Sometimes you cannot name the beneficiary because you do not own the policy.) It also includes property that you can dispose of under an arrangement set up by someone else, if you have what lawyers call a "general power of appointment" over the property.

General powers of appointment may be either "inter vivos" (exercisable during your life) or "testamentary" (exercisable by your will); most general powers are testamentary. If you have a general inter vivos power, you may take the property yourself or use it to pay your debts. If you have a general testamentary power, you have no right to take the property for yourself but you can dispose of it as part of your estate. If you have both kinds of powers, you have as much control over the property as if you owned it outright.

If you have only a "special power of appointment," you can neither take the property yourself nor add it to your estate. Special powers allow you to choose who will receive property, within the limits specified by the person who created the power, but the property is not taxed as part of your estate.

Your taxable estate may also include amounts that are payable under an arrangement set up by an employer or under a retirement arrangement that you set up yourself. Such arrangements are popular ways to provide benefits upon retirement or death.

You also may want to estimate what part of the property that you can dispose of will be included in your "probate estate," in order to estimate the cost of administering your estate. Generally, your "probate estate" refers to property that will have to be transferred by your executor from your name to the names of your beneficiaries, unless your executor sells it to pay debts or taxes. Your probate estate and taxable estate are not necessarily identical. Some of the property that is counted in figuring your estate tax, such as property in joint names that passes to the surviving joint owner or insurance payable to a beneficiary other than your estate, is not part of your probate estate. Whether or not real estate in your name alone is included depends on the law of the state where the real estate is located. Again, your lawyer can give you an estimate of what will be included in your probate estate.

As values of property are constantly changing, for most kinds of property it will not be worth going to the trouble and expense of getting a formal appraisal in order to figure out what you have to work with.

You probably already have a general idea of the value of many of the items you own. In the case of real estate, a broker often will give you, either free of charge or for a small fee, a "ball park" estimate which is accurate enough to use in making your personal financial plan. In the case of unusual items of substantial value, such as art objects or antiques, an appraisal may already have been made for insurance purposes.

The following checklist will help you figure out what property you have to work with in making your financial plan.

Property Owned by You Alone

1. Real estate
    a. The house (or houses) you live in, if in
        your name alone   _____
        Less outstanding balances due under
            any mortgages or trust deeds (used in
            place of mortgages in some states)   _____
        Value of equity (the amount by which
            the value of the house exceeds the
            amount you owe on a mortgage or
            trust deed)   _____
    b. Other real estate   _____
        Less mortgage (or trust deed) balance   _____
        Value of equity   _____

2. Other residential property, if in your name
    alone

    a. Cooperative apartment   ————
       Less outstanding balance due on loan   ————
       Value of equity   ————
    b. Condominium   ————
       Less mortgage (or trust deed) balance   ————
       Value of equity   ————

3. Securities (except stock in a closely held business)
    a. Common stocks   ————
    b. Preferred stocks   ————
    c. Bonds and debentures   ————
    d. Mutual fund shares   ————
    e. Money market fund shares   ————
       Total   ————

4. Debts owed to you by others
    a. Debts secured by mortgage or trust deed   ————
    b. Loans you have made to others   ————
    c. Other debts owed to you   ————
       Total   ————

5. Life insurance
    a. Insurance on your life
       Face amounts payable at death   ————
       Less any outstanding loans   ————
       Net amount payable at your death   ————
    b. Insurance owned by you that is on the life of someone else, such as your husband   ————
       Face amounts   ————
       Less any outstanding loans   ————
       Net amount payable on the death of the insured   ————

6. Accounts at banks and savings institutions
    a. Checking accounts   ————
    b. Savings accounts   ————

    c. Certificates of deposit   _____

    d. Money market accounts   _____

    e. Super NOW accounts   _____

       Total   _____

7. Business interests
    a. Sole proprietorships (businesses that you own individually)   _____
    b. Interests in partnerships   _____
    c. Stock in a closely held business   _____
    d. Other business property, such as patents, copyrights, and contracts providing for payments to be made to you   _____
       Total   _____

8. Personal property
    a. Automobiles   _____
    b. Boats and airplanes   _____
    c. Furniture and rugs   _____
    d. Art objects   _____
    e. Jewelry, table silver, china, glassware   _____
    f. Collections of stamps, coins, or other items   _____
       Total   _____

9. Other property
    a. Gold and silver bars or other interests   _____
    b. Cash—currency and coins   _____
    c. Transferable club memberships   _____
    d. Miscellaneous   _____
       Total   _____
         Grand Total   _____

10. Your debts   _____

You should deduct the amount of any debts payable by you that are not covered in the preceding items.

       Grand Total less your debts   _____

Property Owned Jointly or As Community Property

You should also list separately your interest in any property of the kinds included in the preceding checklist that you own as community property with your husband or jointly with anyone.

There are so many different ways to hold title to property that you may not be able to tell whether it is in your name alone or is held jointly with someone else as tenants in common, joint tenants, or tenants by the entirety. This is particularly true of real estate. When you see your lawyer about your financial plan, he may want to see the deed in order to be sure how the title is held.

Benefits Payable Now, upon Retirement, or at Death

You should also take the following benefits into account:
1. Amounts payable to you under an arrangement set up by your husband, such as life insurance or retirement plan benefits
2. Benefits payable by your employer
3. Benefits provided by a retirement arrangement you set up yourself
4. Social security benefits

19

Property You Can Dispose Of Even Though It Does Not Belong to You

Finally, take into account any property that you have the power to dispose of, even though it is not in your name. Powers of appointment are relevant here. Although such a power may not make you any wealthier, it increases the amount you can dispose of and may influence your decisions regarding property that you do own. For example, suppose you have been married twice and have children from both marriages. Suppose, also, that your first husband's will gives you a special power of appointment which allows you to choose which of his children will receive property that was in his estate. You may use this power to provide for the children from your first marriage and use your own property to provide for the children from your second marriage.

Why You Need Information about Your Husband's Property and Financial Plan

Information regarding your husband's property and financial plan may be crucial to you in making your own plan. Some husbands refuse to share such information. Not only could this make your planning difficult, it could have other repercussions as well. For example, settling your husband's estate could be difficult if neither you nor the executor named in his will has been fully informed about the location of his property and important papers. Should your husband become incapacitated, similar information would be needed by whoever handles his affairs.

Important items for you to know about your husband's property include:

1. What he owns, what it cost, and when he bought it
2. Where he has a safe deposit box and where the key is kept
3. Where his will and other important papers, such as trust agreements, deeds, and tax returns, are kept
4. Names and addresses of his lawyer, broker, investment adviser, accountant, insurance agent, and any other professionals he relies on in financial matters
5. Information about any trusts he has set up or has an interest in
6. Whether he has given anyone a power of attorney

It also is very helpful for you to know how your husband's financial plan disposes of his property. For example, if his will provides that your children will receive sums of money when they reach twenty-one, you may want to delay the time at which they receive money under the terms of your will, so that they will not have more than they can handle responsibly at that age.

My wife and I have shared with each other the information described here. I hope that you and your husband will do likewise, if you have not done so already.

If you are single or widowed, you should consider whether there is someone in particular you wish to keep informed about these matters. If there is not, your executor should be told where to find the information.

CHAPTER 2

How to Make the Tools of Estate Planning Work for You

WILLS are by far the most widely used tool of estate planning. A will can be used to dispose of property upon death, and as most people who make a financial plan do not dispose of everything during their lifetime, few plans are complete without a will. Later, in chapter 10, you will learn what a will can—and cannot—do for you.

This chapter introduces other major estate-planning tools:

1. *Trusts.* Trusts are arrangements that allow one or more individuals or a bank or trust company (or a combination of the two) to hold property for your

benefit or for others you want to help. In disposing of the trust property and the income it produces, the trustees are under a legal duty to follow the terms of the will or agreement that sets up the trust.

Trusts are such an important tool—and may be used in so many different ways—that they are discussed not only in this chapter but throughout the book.

2. *Life insurance, employee benefits, and other retirement arrangements.* These forms of wealth usually provide for payments after your death to people chosen by you, in addition to any benefits that may be paid to you during your lifetime. Like trusts, they may be used in many different ways, and they are discussed throughout this book.

3. *Lifetime gifts.* Gifts may be made either directly to the people you want to help or in trust for them, or, if an individual is under age or mentally incompetent, to a guardian or custodian for his or her benefit. Chapter 7 will discuss how to make gifts of different kinds of property, such as real estate, securities, and tangible personal property, as well as the advantages of making gifts.

4. *Joint ownership.* Holding property jointly in your name and the name of someone else is an important tool of estate planning, but it is not always a desirable arrangement.*

5. *Powers of attorney.* A power of attorney may be used to allow someone else to act in your name to manage your property.

6. *Powers of appointment.* A power of appointment allows the person to whom the power is given (the "donee") to choose ("appoint") who will receive certain property. Usually the power applies to property in a trust, but it sometimes applies to other property, such as land, that is not in trust. The power may be either "special," so that the donee may choose only

*See chapter 4, pp. 75–78.

among members of a limited group, or "general," so that the donee may appoint to anyone, including himself or herself.

For example, your husband's will may provide that on your death, the property in a trust shall go to such of his children as you shall "appoint" by your will. In that case, you, as donee of a special power, can choose which children will get the trust property.

Because powers usually are created in connection with trusts, they are discussed with trusts in chapter 8, on pages 144–46.

7. *Sales, loans, and other methods of helping someone without making a gift.* Tools that allow you to help others financially without making a gift are useful because they often do not require a lawyer and may avoid gift taxes.*

8. *Marriage contracts.* Marriage contracts (what lawyers call "antenuptial agreements") are sometimes used to try to limit the rights a husband may have to his wife's property during the marriage or upon her death, or his rights to alimony or property of hers if the marriage ends in divorce. Husbands also use such contracts to limit the rights of wives. Whether such a contract will be effective in achieving these goals depends on state law.†

Which of these tools may be useful for you depends on the amount of property you have to work with. Tools that are useful for women who have a limited amount of property, and who are mainly concerned with getting someone to manage their property to meet their own needs are discussed in the section beginning on page 38. Tools that are more likely to be useful for women who want to

---

* See chapter 9.
† See p. 67.

provide for others in addition to meeting their own needs are discussed in the section beginning on page 45.

Trusts

Trusts have been used for hundreds of years to provide management of property for people who are unable to take care of it themselves. Trusts can often save taxes as well. Lawyers call the people who may receive money or property from a trust the "beneficiaries." Trusts may be created either by will or "inter vivos" (between the living) by a trust agreement signed by the "grantor," "donor," "settlor," or "trustor" (all four terms refer to the person who creates the trust) and the trustee.

In order to set up a trust, you need someone to act as trustee. The trustee can be a bank or trust company, or one or more individuals. You can, if you wish, have one or more individuals serve with an institution as cotrustee.* You can be a trustee yourself, although if you want to save taxes you often cannot be the sole trustee if the trustees have broad powers.

There are four major kinds of trusts that you may set up to carry out your personal financial plan (the first three are all inter vivos trusts):

1. Revocable ("living") trusts, under which you have

---

*The advantages and disadvantages of various kinds of trustees are discussed in chapter 19 on pp. 270–73.

the power to revoke the trust and take back the trust property

2. Short-term trusts, which provide for the return of the trust property to you after a specified period of time, but which cannot be revoked during that period

3. Irrevocable trusts, under which you have no power to revoke the trust and take back the trust property and which do not provide for the return of the property to you at any time

4. Testamentary trusts, which are created by your will, rather than during your life

Revocable ("living") Trusts

A revocable inter vivos trust (commonly referred to as a "living" trust, because "inter vivos" is Latin for "between the living") is simply an arrangement for managing and disposing of the property of the person who created the trust. Because you have the power to revoke the trust and take back the trust property, you still have control over it whenever you want to exercise that power. In most states, if you want to have the power to revoke, you must specifically say so in the document establishing the trust; otherwise, the trust will be irrevocable and you cannot take back the property.

Usually the person who creates a revocable trust retains the power to revoke without having to get the consent of any other person. Sometimes the trust instrument provides that the consent of another person is needed in order to revoke the trust, but this provision is unusual. If you set up a revocable trust, you should require the consent of another person to revoke only if you feel you cannot rely on your own judgment in the matter or if you are concerned about protecting the trust property from the claims of your creditors.

If you do not use a revocable trust to provide for the management and disposition of your property, you can manage it yourself during your lifetime (as long as you remain legally competent) and can then dispose of it by will. So revocable trusts and wills are alternative ways to dispose of property. Each has its own advantages and disadvantages.*

Short-Term Trusts

Short-term trusts provide for the return of the trust property to the person who set it up, after a specified period of time. Short-term trusts are used to save income taxes by causing income from the trust property to be taxed either to a beneficiary who is in a lower tax bracket than the person who created the trust or to the trust itself as a separate taxpayer. A short-term trust must last a minimum of ten years and one day or for the life of the beneficiary who gets the income, whichever ends first, or the trust will be ignored for income tax purposes and the income taxed to the person who set up the trust.

Short-term trusts are primarily useful if you are in a high income tax bracket and would like to save taxes by temporarily shifting the income from some of your property to someone else, but do not want to give up the property permanently.†

---

* For a discussion, see chapter 10 (wills); chapter 11 (revocable trusts).
† Short-term trusts are discussed in more detail in chapter 8, pp. 138–40.

Irrevocable Trusts

Irrevocable inter vivos trusts are also set up during the life of the person who creates the trust, often to save taxes. An irrevocable trust, however, does *not* give the person who created the trust the power to revoke it and get the trust property back. Unless you are satisfied that you will not change your mind after you have created the trust, you should not set up an irrevocable trust.

Three kinds of irrevocable trusts are important in financial planning:

1. Long-term trusts
2. Present interest trusts, which fit the definition of a "present interest," so that gifts made through the trust, up to $10,000 each year, are exempt from the gift tax
3. Charitable split-interest trusts, which provide benefits for both an individual and a charitable organization

Long-term trusts may save both income and estate taxes. Usually, if you go to the trouble and expense of setting up a trust, you want it to last longer than the minimum time required to keep you from being taxed on the income of a short-term trust, so that the tax advantages and other benefits the trust may provide will last longer. However, the important feature is not how long the trust lasts, but rather that it prohibits returning any of the trust property to the person who set up the trust.

Long-term trusts are primarily useful for wealthier women who want to save estate taxes as well as income taxes and who are satisfied that they can give away part of their money and never miss it.*

Present interest trusts are primarily useful for women who want to make gifts of limited amounts to their children or grandchildren without actually turning over the money to them.† These trusts may save income, estate, and gift taxes. They are a kind of irrevocable trust that take their name from the so-called present interest exclusion‡ in the gift tax. The exclusion allows certain types of gifts of up to $10,000 per year to each recipient to be exempt for both gift tax and estate tax purposes. If you are married and your husband gives his consent so that you can use his exclusion as well as yours, the amount can be doubled, allowing you to give $20,000 to each recipient.

A present interest trust is simply one kind of irrevocable trust. As such, it must prohibit having the trust property return to the person who set up the trust.

Charitable split-interest trusts are primarily useful for wealthy women or women who have few relatives to provide for,§ because most women want to use the bulk of their wealth to provide for their own families, rather than for charity. These trusts may save income, estate, and gift taxes. Their most impor-

---

*Long-term trusts are covered in more detail in chapter 8, pp. 140–47.

†Present interest trusts are discussed in chapter 8, pp. 130–35.

‡The tax rules for this exclusion are covered in chapter 14, pp. 223–24.

§Charitable split-interest trusts are discussed in chapter 8, pp. 147–51.

tant feature is that they provide for both a charitable and a noncharitable beneficiary. For example, you may create a trust to make regular payments to your daughter during her life. When she dies, the trust property (and any accumulated income) would go to a named charity. You may even create a charitable split-interest trust to make regular payments to you, but you must prohibit the return of the trust property to you. You may also reverse the order and have the trust make regular payments to a named charity for a period of years and then have the trust property go to your child or grandchild.

Testamentary Trusts

A testamentary trust is an arrangement created by the will of the testator (the person who made the will) to manage and dispose of property after he or she dies. For example, you may provide in your will that property left to your children shall be held for their benefit by a trustee.

Testamentary trusts are created for a variety of reasons. Frequently, the testator wants to leave property for the benefit of a young child who is not able to handle it. Taxes may also be an important reason to create a testamentary trust, to qualify for the special estate tax marital deduction for property that goes to a surviving husband (or wife) or the charitable deduction for property that goes to a qualified charity. It is not necessary to use a trust to obtain these deductions, but there may be important advantages in doing so.*

---

*For a discussion of different kinds of trusts that may be used for this purpose, see chapter 12, pp. 198–200.

Trusts also may be used to keep the present spouse of a beneficiary, or anyone the beneficiary may marry in the future, from sharing property that is part of an estate.

Life Insurance, Employee Benefits, and Other Retirement Arrangements

Life insurance, employee benefits, individual retirement arrangements—IRAs and HR 10 (Keogh) plans—are forms of wealth that can also be important estate-planning tools. They usually include benefits which after your death will be paid to people you have chosen, in addition to any benefits paid to you during your lifetime.

Life Insurance

Life insurance is particularly important for younger women who do not have substantial amounts of property because it offers a way to create an "instant estate." When the first premium is paid, a fund is created that will provide for your survivors as long as the policy is in force. The peace of mind that protection brings may be worth many times the premiums paid.

The two major forms of life insurance are term and ordinary (or "whole") life. Term insurance provides coverage for a fixed period only and may specify that the policy can then be renewed or converted into ordinary life insurance. Unless renewed or converted, a term insurance policy ceases to have any value once the period of time that it covers has expired. While the policy is in force, any cash surrender value the policy may have will be constantly declining.

The value of ordinary life insurance, on the other hand, builds up, so that you can surrender the policy to the insurance company for cash or use it as security for a loan from the company. Thus, it is a form of investment and may be kept in force by timely payment of premiums as long as you live. Sometimes the policy may provide that premiums are payable only for a limited period—for example, for twenty years, or until the insured reaches age sixty-five.

Unfortunately, some insurance that is sold is not a good buy from the standpoint of you and your beneficiaries. This is so for two reasons: first, the agent's commission represents a large part of the first year's premium and continues in later years, often at a rate substantially higher than for other types of investment assets; and second, you may buy ordinary life when you would be much better served with term insurance.

One good way to keep down the cost of meeting your insurance needs is to shop around and compare the different policies that are available to you. In some states, savings banks offer insurance that is a relatively good buy because they pay no commissions to agents and have lower selling expenses. Your employer may provide group term insurance coverage, either at no cost to you or at a reasonable premium, and may allow you to take out additional coverage as well.

Another good way to keep down the cost of your insurance is to buy term policies, rather than ordinary life. As indicated, term policies are designed merely to cover the risk that the insured will die during the period the policy is in force, not to build up an investment. For many women and their husbands, insurance against the risk of dying in the near future, before they have accumulated an estate and while they still have young children to be raised and educated, makes good sense. That protection is best provided by term insurance.

Ordinary life, however, gives the insurance company additional funds to invest to build up the cash surrender and loan value of the policy over the years. Although the premiums are higher at first than for term insurance, they do not go up as the years pass, the way term insurance premiums do as the insured gets older. If you believe that you will continue to want insurance coverage over the long haul, ordinary life has the advantage of keeping the premiums at a more affordable level. Whether that is a desirable way to handle your savings depends on your individual needs and temperament, as well as on how liberal the insurance company is in paying dividends to policyholders.

Insurance companies as a group have an excellent record for meeting their dollar obligations to policyholders. They have not been as successful in keeping up with inflation. Most policies are for fixed amounts and most insurance company investments are in bonds and mortgages, rather than stocks or real estate. It is only in recent years that interest rates on bonds and mortgages have been high enough to reflect inflation and to offer returns comparable to those which have been available from stocks or real estate.

During periods when stock prices are increasing, it generally has paid young people to buy term insurance and to use the difference between the term insurance premiums and the higher premiums they would have paid on whole life policies to buy stocks, or shares in a mutual fund that invests in stocks. However, stock prices can fall substantially, and the mutual funds generally have failed to sell stocks prior to these declines. So these alternative investments do involve major risks. Also, many people find it difficult to save and invest on a regular basis and like the stimulus provided by having to pay premiums on an ordinary life insurance policy, even though another investment might be more profitable, because they fear that the premium dollars saved by buying term insurance would be spent instead of being saved and invested.

An informative booklet on buying life insurance is the "Consumers' Union Report on Life Insurance: Plan and Buy Wisely" (4th ed., 1980), available for $9.25 from Consumer Reports Books, P.O. Box C719, Brooklyn, NY 11205.

Employee Benefits, Individual Retirement Arrangements (IRAs), and HR 10 (Keogh) Plans

Three major tools of estate planning offer unusual opportunities to accumulate and transfer wealth without paying taxes at the usual rates:

1. Qualified employee benefit plans
2. Individual retirement arrangements (IRAs)
3. HR 10 (Keogh) plans

All three allow the employer or employee who sets aside money for retirement and death benefits to get an income tax deduction when the money is set aside, but the employee (or the person who receives the death benefit) isn't taxed until the money is paid out. The entire amount set aside for the employee can earn income for his or her benefit. If the amount had been paid to the employee instead, only the money remaining after the payment of income tax could be invested. In addition, no tax is due on the income from the money set aside until it is paid out. In the meantime, the income can accumulate tax free.

If you are in a qualified plan, this postponement of income taxes can be a tremendous advantage to you for two reasons: It is like getting an interest-free loan from the United States Treasury—the effect is the same as if you paid your tax and the government immediately loaned you the amount of tax that you had paid, without charging you interest on the loan; and you, or your beneficiary, may be in a lower tax bracket when the money is paid out than the bracket you were in when the money was set aside by your employer.

If you are employed, you can set up your own individual retirement arrangement (IRA) and get similar advantages. However, there are very technical rules for both qualified plans and IRAs, as well as limits on the amounts that you can set aside. Your lawyer can guide you through the maze of rules.

If you are self-employed, your lawyer can advise you about setting up an HR 10 (Keogh) plan, which is generally like "qualified" plans set up by other employers but, again, is subject to special rules and restrictions.

When you set up a plan, you should bear in mind that your contributions generally cannot be withdrawn until you retire, unless you are willing to pay heavy additional taxes. Your contributions may be moved from one form of investment to another as long as you are careful to follow the tax rules. For example, you can withdraw money invested in a mutual fund and invest it in a bank savings account instead.

Qualified Plans Set Up by Employers. The major kinds of qualified plans that employers set up include pension, profit sharing, incentive stock option, and stock bonus plans. These plans are often referred to as "savings" or "thrift" plans. They usually provide a monthly retirement income to the employee.

If your employer has a qualified plan, it may provide for payments to your beneficiary after your death. A typical plan would give you and your beneficiary a variety of options as to how benefits are paid. As the tax rules governing benefits under qualified plans are highly technical, your lawyer should review your plan to be sure that it is properly handled in disposing of your estate.

Under the tax law, some employers are allowed to offer their employees the opportunity to set up a "tax-deferred annuity": Amounts are withheld from employees' salaries and invested for them and are used to make regular payments to them when they retire. If you want to save income taxes and your employer has such a plan, this is a good way to do it, because the money withheld isn't taxed until you collect it. You should check first to see whether there are any restrictions on the time that you can cash in the annuity.

Individual Retirement Arrangements (IRAs). If you are employed, you may set up an individual retirement arrangement (IRA), regardless of whether your employer has a qualified plan for employees. The most common arrangements are with a bank, savings and loan association, or mutual fund. In order to set one up, you sign a form furnished by the institution and may invest each year a maximum of $2,000, or, if your earned income is less than that, an amount equal to your earned income.

Your husband can also set up an IRA for himself. If your husband has no earned income, you may be able to set up a second IRA for him, but the combined investment each year may not exceed $2,250 or your earned income, whichever is less. If you have no earned income but your husband does, he can set up an IRA for you and the same rules apply. The amount put into the plan, up to these limits, is deductible for income tax purposes.

As with a qualified plan, the income earned on the money you invest is not taxed until it is paid to you or your beneficiary. Detailed rules are provided by law as to when payments must begin upon your retirement or death and how soon they must be completed.

For an informative booklet dealing with IRAs and other aspects of planning for retirement, see "The IRA Book," available for $5.95 from the Center for the Study of Services, 1518 K Street, N.W., Suite 406, Washington, D.C. 20005.

HR 10 (Keogh) Plans. If you are in a business or profession in which you do not work for anyone else, you will not be covered by a regular qualified plan for employees. However, you may set up an HR 10 (Keogh) plan for yourself and any employees you may have. These plans bear the name of the Congressman who introduced House Resolution 10 to allow qualified pension and profit-sharing plans to cover self-employed individuals. The limit on the amount you can invest each year in an HR 10 plan is $30,000 or 25 percent of your earned income, whichever is less.

If you do not have employees in your business, an HR 10 plan is relatively simple to set up. Complications enter in if you have employees, as the law requires that the plan not discriminate against them and in your favor.

Suppose you are employed by someone else but also have a business or profession of your own. In that situation, you may be covered both by your employer's plan and by your own HR 10 plan for your business or profession (or for each of your businesses, if you have more than one).

Tools to Use If You Want Your Money Managed to Meet Your Own Needs

Let's begin with Mary Smith, an elderly woman with a limited amount of property who is mainly concerned with providing for her own needs. Because of Mary's poor health and impending move to a nursing home (or into her daughter's home), she wants an arrangement that will allow her property to be managed for her benefit by her married daughter, Ruth Jones. What are Mary's options in setting up such an arrangement? She has four major alternatives:

1. She can simply transfer her property to Ruth and rely on Ruth to use it for her benefit.
2. She can put her property in joint names with Ruth.
3. She can leave her property in her own name, but give Ruth a power of attorney.
4. She can create a revocable ("living") trust with Ruth as trustee.

Gift or Outright Transfer

Many women in Mary's situation have simply transferred their property to someone else to allow that person to manage the property for them. In some cases this may be a satisfactory arrangement, particularly if the amount transferred is not so large as to require payment of a substantial gift tax. However, there are major risks involved. If Mary transfers her property to Ruth, it is now legally Ruth's and Mary is forced to rely on Ruth's willingness to use it for her benefit. Even if Mary has complete confidence that Ruth can be relied on to do this, other risks remain.

The arrangement makes Mary completely dependent on Ruth, which may have a bad effect on the way Mary and Ruth feel about each other. If Ruth owes money, her creditors may try to get paid from the property that was originally Mary's. And if the unexpected happens and Ruth dies before Mary, all of Ruth's property will be disposed of by her will (or by state law applicable to people who die without a valid will). That may mean that property which originally belonged to Mary will pass to Ruth's husband (if she is married) or to any children she may leave, if Ruth fails to make a will leaving to Mary everything that came from her. If Ruth does make such a will, her husband usually has the right under state law to claim a share without regard to what her will provides. There also may be estate and inheritance taxes to be paid, if Ruth owns enough property when she dies, which may reduce the amount that is returned to Mary.

Joint Ownership

Often someone in Mary's situation will put some or all of her property in joint names with Ruth. In the case of checking and savings accounts, this may be a desirable arrangement. It permits Ruth to withdraw funds from the joint account to pay Mary's bills, and yet avoids some of the risks that follow from an outright transfer.

Depending on state law, Ruth's creditors may or may not be able to get paid from money Mary put into the joint account. There are different types of joint accounts, and the language used in the agreement with the bank is important. If Ruth dies before Mary, Ruth's husband or her heirs ordinarily would have no claim to money in the account, and it would all belong to Mary. So Mary's risk of losing her money is less than in an outright transfer to Ruth.

Assuming that Mary dies before Ruth, however,

Ruth may be entitled to the balance in the account as surviving joint depositor. This keeps any other children from getting a share of the money in the account. But, depending on state law and on which bank form is used, Ruth may not be entitled to the balance in the account if she merely had the power to sign checks for Mary's convenience and not to make herself co-owner of the account. If this is the arrangement Mary wants, she should be sure to sign the appropriate bank form.

The convenience of the joint account may be important, if Mary's social security and other checks are deposited in the account and can thus be drawn against without requiring Mary's endorsement to deposit them. Although there is always the possibility that Ruth will withdraw money for her own purposes instead of for Mary's bills, the amount subject to this risk at any given time may be small if Mary keeps the balance in the account low.

Joint ownership of securities or of Mary's home is less likely to be a desirable arrangement if Mary's goal is merely to allow her property to be used for her benefit without having to sign each time this is done. In order to sell real estate or securities in joint names, it is necessary for Mary to sign as well as Ruth. Again, other children may be cut out of their shares of the property.

Powers of Attorney

Giving a power of attorney is a way for one person to authorize another to sign checks, legal papers, tax returns, and other documents in his or her name. For example, if Mary gives Ruth a power of attorney, prepared by Mary's lawyer, Ruth would then be able to sign legal papers for Mary, using a phrase such as: "Mary Smith by Ruth Jones, attorney in fact." If Mary wants Ruth to be able to sign for her in dealing with her property, a power of attorney may appear to be a good way to achieve that result.

Whether a power of attorney will allow Ruth to deal effectively with Mary's property for Mary's benefit depends on several factors. In some states, the power automatically ceases to be effective just when it may be needed most, when Mary becomes mentally incompetent. In recent years, however, most states have changed this rule to allow "durable" powers of attorney to be executed by a person in Mary's situation while she is still mentally competent. The durable power will continue to be valid if she later ceases to be competent. It should be prepared by a lawyer and signed before a notary. The durable power, then, can authorize Ruth to sign various kinds of documents for Mary and to manage a group of securities and bank accounts for her, even if Mary becomes incompetent at some point after signing the power.

If the state in which Mary lives authorizes such durable powers of attorney, it may be a useful tool for Mary. However, even in such a state, some persons or institutions may be unwilling to rely on Ruth's power, if much time has gone by since Mary signed it and she has not renewed it by signing another. Banks may also insist that their own power of attorney card be signed for bank accounts. For these reasons, a revocable trust may be needed to provide a more comprehensive and lasting arrangement to allow Ruth, or another trustee, to act on Mary's behalf and to manage her property for her benefit should she become incompetent.

Revocable Trusts

Trusts may be for the benefit of anyone, including the grantor who creates the trust. A trust that can be revoked by the grantor, so that the trust property is returned by the trustee just as if no trust had been created, may serve many purposes.* Those discussed here are likely to be important both for women with a limited amount of property, like Mary, and for those with more substantial assets.

Whether Mary should create a revocable trust depends on whether it makes sense for her to bear the additional expense of setting up a trust in order to achieve the benefits it may provide for her and for the people she wants to help financially.

If Mary decides to create a revocable trust, she should have a lawyer prepare a trust agreement, to be signed by her as grantor and by Ruth as trustee. Then Mary can transfer property to Ruth as trustee under the trust agreement, rather than to her individually. Ruth will be legally obligated to follow Mary's directions in the trust agreement in disposing of property she holds as trustee.

The agreement can provide that the property must be used by Ruth for Mary's benefit during her lifetime, and that any that remains when she dies will be divided between Mary's children or grandchildren (or whomever else she may wish to name).

---

* The full range of purposes that may be served by a revocable trust is covered in chapter 11.

Ruth cannot use the trust property for her own benefit unless the trust agreement says she may do this, and her creditors cannot take the trust property to pay her debts.

A revocable trust is particularly useful in states that do not authorize the use of "durable" powers of attorney because Ruth's power to act as trustee and to use the trust property for Mary's benefit will continue even if Mary becomes legally incompetent.

A revocable trust, however, serves purposes in addition to those served by a durable power. Even if a power of attorney does not become ineffective if the person who gave the power becomes legally incompetent, it does lose its effectiveness when that person dies. So a power of attorney cannot take the place of a will and be used to dispose of a person's property after he or she dies. In contrast, a revocable trust, although not a complete substitute for a will, can dispose of whatever property is in the trust after the death of the grantor. To that extent, the revocable trust does indeed take the place of a will.

In Mary's case, then, the trust can provide that any property remaining in the trust when Mary dies will be divided among her children or grandchildren, just as if she had made a will leaving that property to them.

Even if Mary uses a revocable trust, she will need a will as well, to dispose of any property that is not in the trust when she dies, and to name an executor.* In addition, a power of attorney is useful to authorize Ruth to sign such legal papers as tax returns, which she cannot do simply by virtue of being trustee.

*See chapter 10, pp. 171–73.

Tools to Use If You Want to Provide for Others

Let's take the case of Louise, a widowed or divorced grandmother with a substantial amount of property. She is mainly concerned with providing for her children and grandchildren, as she has more money than she expects to need herself. She may want to use the same estate-planning tools that Mary might use, but often in different ways and for different purposes. And there are other tools that are not well adapted to Mary's situation but that may be useful to Louise in carrying out her personal financial plan. For example, Louise may make gifts during her life to an irrevocable trust for the benefit of her children and grandchildren.

Although Louise has more than enough for her own needs, in dealing with the money she expects to use for those needs her situation may be similar to Mary's. She, too, may want to arrange for part of her money to be managed for her benefit, instead of leaving it all in her own name and having to manage it herself. Of course, Louise, like Mary, needs a will to dispose of any property that is in her name when she dies, and to name an executor.

For Louise, then, the most appropriate arrangement may include both a power of attorney and a revocable trust, to serve one or more of the purposes discussed in chapter 11.

CHAPTER 3

How to Keep Taxes, Costs, and Husbands from Blocking Your Plan

WHAT can keep your personal financial plan from working full time for you and the people you want to help? The three most important roadblocks are taxes, costs, and husbands.

Taxes may affect every woman, married or single. The first section of this chapter describes the taxes you must deal with: four federal taxes—income, estate, gift, and generation-skipping transfer taxes—as well as state and local taxes. The section also suggests how you can go about reducing these taxes.

For a woman with a limited amount of property, the cost of the professional services needed to make and carry out her plan may be a more important factor than taxes. These costs include fees of lawyers and other professionals, brokers' commissions and other expenses connected with investments, trustees' fees if she sets up a trust, and the expenses involved in settling her estate. When you invest—whether it is in securities, mutual fund shares, real estate, or life insurance—you may incur a commission or sales charge. Even if, as with life insurance, no commission appears on the premium statement, it is an expense for the company that is reflected in the premium you are charged for the policy. The same costs also affect women with more substantial amounts of property, even if they do not loom as large in relation to taxes. The second section of this chapter analyzes the costs that may be incurred in carrying out your plan and discusses how you might keep these costs down.

Husbands also deserve a place on the list of roadblocks because state law usually allows your husband, if he survives you, to claim a share of your estate no matter what you provide in your will. In the eight community property states—Arizona, California, Idaho, Louisiana, Nevada, New Mexico, Texas, and Washington—husbands and wives each own half of the community property, which includes whatever either of you saves from your earnings while you are married. His half of the community property is his to dispose of even if he dies before you do, and the same is true for you if you are the first to die. The final section suggests ways to reduce the risk that your husband will assert his rights in a way that disrupts your personal financial plan.

47

Taxes and You

Your personal financial plan may be affected by federal, state, and local taxes. However, many women with limited amounts of property worry more about taxes than they need to, because their income and wealth is not large enough to incur any substantial tax (other than the local property tax).

Federal Taxes

The four federal taxes that may be important in making your financial plan are:

1. Income tax
2. Estate tax
3. Gift tax
4. Generation-skipping transfer tax

Income Tax. Almost all women are familiar with the federal income tax. What many do not realize is how much can be done through sound financial planning to reduce the tax they pay. Two important ways are to postpone the time when the tax is due and to make income taxable to another member of your family (or someone else you are interested in helping financially) who is in a lower income tax bracket than you are.

There are many ways to postpone the time when income taxes are due. For example, chapter 2 (pages 37–38) showed how you may be able to set up a retirement plan (an IRA or a Keogh plan) which will allow you to deduct money from your taxable income each year and not pay tax on the money until you withdraw it from the plan. Meanwhile, the money set aside under the plan is invested to produce income which also is not taxed until it is withdrawn. The result is that you have an interest-free loan from the government in the amount of the tax that you would have paid if you had not set up the plan.

Another way to save income taxes is to make income taxable to someone in your family (or someone else who you want to help) who is in a lower tax bracket than you are. For example, if Ruth is helping to support her mother, Mary, Ruth can do this in either of two ways: She can earn money or get income from her investments, pay income tax on it at her rates, and then give what is left to Mary; or she can set up a trust, transfer some of her securities to the trust, and provide that the trust income shall be paid to Mary. If the trust will last either for at least ten years or for Mary's life, and if it satisfies other tax rules that Congress has laid down, then the trust income paid to Mary will be taxed as her income rather than as Ruth's. If Mary is in a lower tax bracket and, therefore, pays taxes at a lower rate than Ruth, there may be enough of a saving to make it worthwhile to set up the trust.*

Estate Tax. This tax is generally based on the amount that an individual owns or has full control over at death, plus certain gifts that he or she had made while alive. The rates are graduated, like the income tax, and increase as the size of the estate increases. However, there is a credit set by Congress

* Using trusts to save income taxes is discussed in more detail in chapter 13, pp. 212–15.

which may reduce, or even cancel out, the estate tax otherwise due. This means that even a substantial estate can be transferred tax free to anyone you may choose. For deaths in the year 1984, the tax credit covers an estate of $325,000. The tax-free amount increases each year from 1985 to 1987, as shown by the following chart:

Year	Tax-Free Amount
1985	$400,000
1986	$500,000
1987 or afterward	$600,000

In addition to this tax-free amount, any part of the estate that passes to a husband or wife in a form that meets the requirements of the special "marital deduction" for gifts to a spouse is also tax free.

Once you are over the tax-free amount, you are subject to tax rates of more than 30 percent. So for a woman who has a million dollar estate, the estate tax is a major roadblock, which may easily take one-fourth of her property or more, if she dies without having taken steps to minimize it.*

Your estate is legally liable for the federal estate tax and your executor is responsible for paying it. If property that is included in your taxable estate does not come into your executor's hands, the people who receive the property may be legally obligated to pay your executor their pro rata share of the tax, unless your will frees them from this obligation. For example, federal law imposes this obligation on people who receive property over which you had a gen-

*See chapter 15.

eral power of appointment, and in certain other situations as well. State law often applies in situations not covered by the federal provisions. Your lawyer can advise you as to how the payment of the estate tax should be provided for in your situation.

Gift Tax. This tax is generally based on the total gifts an individual makes over the course of his or her life, from the time the present gift tax law became effective in 1932. The tax-free amount is the same as for the federal estate tax: $325,000 in 1984, increasing each year from 1985 to 1987, when it will be $600,000.

Although the tax-free amount is the same for the estate tax and the gift tax, that does not mean that you can give $600,000 tax free in 1987 and leave another $600,000 free of estate tax when you die. All lifetime gifts made after 1976 that count for purposes of the gift tax are added back to determine the amount taxable when you die. In the example just given, the taxable estate would be $1,200,000, and only $600,000 of that amount would be tax free.

Gifts from one person to another which do not exceed $10,000 in any year generally are covered by the "annual exclusion" and do not count for either gift tax or estate tax purposes. For example, if you give your daughter $10,000, the gift will not count for gift tax purposes if it is what lawyers call a "present interest"—the kind of gift that provides immediate rights to the recipient as soon as the gift is made. It would not matter that your daughter may have received similar $10,000 gifts from other people. She does not have to pay income tax on any of her gifts unless what she is given is income from a trust, for example. Such $10,000 gifts do not count for estate tax purposes when you die, unless you make a gift of insurance on your life and die within three years of making the gift.

If the gift is more than $10,000, only the excess counts for gift tax and estate tax purposes. For example, if you give your daughter $40,000 and the gift is a present interest, so that the $10,000 annual exclusion applies, only $30,000 would use up part of the lifetime tax-free amount described above and also count toward the tax-free amount at your death.

Gift tax rates are graduated, like the estate tax, and increase in size as the total gifts made during the donor's lifetime increases. There are a number of ways to minimize gift taxes.* You, as donor, are legally liable to pay the tax, although gifts are sometimes made with the understanding that the recipient will pay it instead.

Generation-Skipping Transfer Tax. This tax was just introduced in 1976. It is extremely complicated to deal with, and there is strong sentiment either to repeal it or to defer its effective date. It is chiefly important for individuals who set up trusts for two or more generations of their descendants. For example, if Louise set up a trust under which income was payable to her daughter Jennie for life, and then on Jennie's death the principal would go to Jennie's children, the trust would not be subject to estate tax on Jennie's death, because all she had was the right to income for her life and that right died with her. In effect, the trust property skips Jennie's generation

* See chapter 14.

(except for income payable to Jennie) and passes to her children in the next generation. The generation-skipping transfer tax is intended to keep the estate tax from being avoided in this way, by imposing a tax when the trust property passes on to the grand-children's generation. But there are ways to cut down the bite of this tax.* The tax is payable by the trustee or other person in possession of property subject to the tax.

State and Local Taxes

Generally, the state taxes that may be important for your personal financial plan are similar to the four federal taxes that have been described, al-though there are differences among the states in the kinds of taxes that are imposed. About half of the states differ from the federal government in having both an inheritance tax, based on the size of each beneficiary's share of an estate, and an estate tax. Others follow the federal government and rely en-tirely on an estate tax, based on the total size of the estate. However, your estate is allowed to deduct amounts paid to the state, up to specified limits, from the federal estate tax. If the deduction allowed for state taxes will be large enough to cover the total paid to the state, which will be the case in many states, the state death taxes can be ignored in making your personal financial plan.

Most states do not tax gifts. People in those states who make gifts to save federal estate taxes enjoy the additional advantage of saving state estate and inher-

*See chapter 16, pp. 249–52.

itance taxes without having to pay any state gift tax to do so.

Many state income taxes are generally similar to the federal income tax. Shifting income to another taxpayer in a lower bracket may save state income taxes, just as it may save federal income taxes.

The local taxes that are most likely to affect your personal financial plan are the property tax, which in some states applies—usually at a reduced rate—to intangible property such as securities, and any city income tax imposed by the city in which you either live or work.

Costs of Professional Services

Who are the professionals whose services you may need to make and carry out your plan, what does each of them do, and how do they charge for their work? My list includes:

1. Lawyers
2. Accountants
3. Brokers
4. Investment managers
5. Insurance agents
6. Custodians of securities
7. Trustees and executors
8. Financial planning consultants

It is important to know what kinds of help each type of professional may be expected to provide.

Lawyers

Lawyers are first on my list, not merely because I am one myself, but because you will need them in so many ways when you make and carry out your personal financial plan. You need a lawyer to buy or sell real estate, to make a will, or to create a trust. You are likely to find a lawyer helpful when you develop your personal plan, because you will want an overview of your financial situation from a legal standpoint. A lawyer can advise you what property will be included in your taxable estate and in your probate estate. You can also obtain advice on minimizing the costs of other professional services you may need. Finally, unless the person you name as your executor is also a lawyer, one will be needed to settle your estate.

In many parts of the country, fees for lawyers for settling estates are set either by law or by generally followed custom in the community, usually on the basis of the value of estate assets. Sometimes it is possible for an executor to negotiate fees lower than those provided by law or by the local fee schedule, if the fees would otherwise be excessive in relation to the work involved. However, if a bank or trust company is named as executor, it often will not be aggressive in seeking to negotiate such a reduction, as it has a natural interest in maintaining a good relationship with the local bar. A family member or friend who is named as executor, either individually or with a bank, is sometimes in a better position to negotiate an appropriate fee.

A lawyer is needed to prepare your will so that it is written in precise legal terms. If your personal financial plan includes a will or trust agreement that is not clearly written, a lawyer may be needed to explain what the document means to the people who must carry out the plan. In some instances, the lack of clarity may be great enough to require court proceedings to settle questions as to the rights of people named in the document or the powers of the executor or trustee responsible for carrying out its provisions.

Lawyers' time is an expensive commodity, and, obviously the expense increases if your will or trust agreement is so unclear as to require court proceedings. Depending on state law, each interested party may also be entitled to be represented by a lawyer at the expense of the estate or trust, multiplying the expense.

As with doctors or other professionals, an ounce of prevention is worth a pound of cure. If you have your personal financial plan prepared by a well-qualified lawyer who does a careful job, the chances that a lawyer will be needed to determine what the plan means are greatly reduced.

Accountants

Accountants prepare financial statements and tax returns. You may be accustomed to preparing your own income tax return and feel no need for an accountant's help in doing so. Returns for estates and trusts are another matter, because of the complex rules that apply to them. Usually, a bank or other professional executor or trustee will undertake to prepare any necessary income tax returns for the estates or trusts it administers, but a separate charge may be made for this service. In most cases, individual executors and trustees are well advised to turn the job over to a professional if the financial affairs of the estate or trust are at all complicated. Even if the individual is able to master the maze of Internal Revenue Code provisions and Treasury regulations that are relevant for this purpose, his time probably is better spent doing something else. I speak from experience, having prepared a number of returns for some small trusts that did not seem to justify the expense of paying a professional to do the job, but took an unreasonable amount of my own time as a result.

If you use a trust as part of your personal financial plan, you should assume that at some point the tax returns for the trust will have to be prepared by a professional. If you expect that the trust will be too small to bear that expense, it probably should not be created to begin with. At a minimum, there should be a provision allowing someone to end the trust if its continued operation becomes impractical or uneconomic.

Brokers

Brokers act for you in buying and selling various kinds of property and are compensated by commissions. Real estate brokers normally represent the seller and charge the seller but not the buyer, who usually deals directly with the seller's broker. In the purchase and sale of securities that are traded on a stock exchange, on the other hand, usually both the buyer and the seller have a broker, each of whom charges a commission. There are wide variations among brokers in the amounts charged.

Sometimes no commission is shown on the broker's statement because the price includes a profit for the broker. This is true of newly issued securities and often for securities traded "over the counter." In the latter case, the price may be marked up substantially over what a selling customer would receive for the same security.

Too many people do not give sufficient thought to minimizing the commissions or other sales charges that they incur in buying and selling property. For example, real estate brokers often charge a commission of 6 percent or more for selling property that the owners might be able to sell as readily themselves. When my mother wanted to sell her house, my sister and I handled the sale without paying a broker's commission, even though we lived in other parts of the country and had to make many of the arrangements by long distance telephone. We paid a broker $60 to appraise the property and ran an ad in the local paper, complete with a photograph of the house. We spent two days showing the house to prospective buyers, and in the process my sister even managed to sell several pieces of furniture that were no longer needed. Although we might have gotten a higher price through a broker, we are satisfied that any difference would have been less than the commission my mother would have had to pay.

If you do not want to sell your property yourself, you may be able to negotiate a reduction in the commission initially quoted by the broker. This is particularly important for unimproved land and commercial property which may be more difficult for you to sell yourself than a house.

The possibilities for obtaining reduced commissions are more clearly defined with securities brokers because there are "discount" brokers who advertise in the financial pages. Their charges may be substantially lower than those of regular brokers, but you should note any differences in the services they provide. Discount brokers do not offer investment advice and may not offer the full range of custodial and financial services provided by other brokers. But if you prefer to make your own purchase and sale decisions rather than relying on a broker for advice, it makes good sense to get a discount from the broker who executes your orders.

In addition to advice, nondiscount brokers may provide accounting data and periodic computations of the market value of securities in an account, and may undertake to keep cash balances invested to produce interest. However, some discount brokers also provide these services. Some nondiscount brokers charge an investment management fee for giving advice, in addition to commissions on purchases and sales.

Whichever kind of broker you choose, you should be satisfied that the services you receive are worth the charges, including commissions, that you incur.

There is a major problem in relying on brokers for advice. The way a broker makes money is through commissions on purchases and sales. This can readily lead to a bias in favor of recommending switches from one investment to another, as the broker earns nothing from your account if you merely continue to hold the same securities. Sometimes switching investments is a sound move. But ideally the decision to switch or to hold should be made by someone who is as neutral as possible, and not by someone motivated by the desire to earn commissions. If you use a discount broker, this problem will not arise, as no recommendations will be made by the broker. It will be entirely up to you tp give purchase and sale orders.

Investment Managers

Investment managers (often referred to as investment counsel) either advise you on when and what securities to buy or sell or act for you in making purchases and sales, usually through brokers. The second procedure is increasingly common, because managers prefer not to have to get in touch with each client when purchases or sales are made. This procedure also allows faster action, which may be important if prices are changing rapidly.

Investment managers attempt to achieve neutrality in making buy and sell recommendations by charging fees based on a percentage of the value of assets under management, often 3/4 percent or 1 percent per year, rather than brokerage commissions. Of course, if the manager is part of or connected with a brokerage firm, this neutrality is not achieved.

Neutrality also may be lacking if the investment manager is under obligation to a particular brokerage firm for one reason or another. For example, I once was looking for an investment manager for a trust. A broker introduced me to several investment managers, with the obvious expectation that the manager I chose would reward the broker by placing orders with him for the trust's account.

Insurance Agents

Your personal financial plan is likely to include one or more forms of insurance coverage, such as life, property, or liability insurance. An insurance agent arranges for this coverage and is compensated by commissions from the insurance company. Ideally, the agent should advise you as to the kind and amount of coverage that you need. Agents vary greatly in the ways they discharge this responsibility. The way they are compensated creates a natural bias in favor of recommending that you buy more different kinds of insurance, and in larger amounts. After getting whatever advice the agent offers, it is up to you to make your own decision as to the coverage you need.

Custodians of Securities

A custodian of securities keeps your stock certificates, bonds, and other relevant papers, collects dividends and interest, delivers securities after you sell them, and often also keeps records needed for income tax purposes. Many brokers will provide most of these services without an additional charge, if you maintain an account for purchases and sales of securities. Although brokers sometimes have gone bankrupt, with unfortunate results for people who had left securities in the broker's custody, there is now federal insurance against such losses up to $400,000 for securities and $100,000 for cash balances. Such insurance safeguards you as a customer against ulti-mate loss from any financial problems of the broker, but there may be a delay before your securities (or their value) are replaced. Some people prefer to have their securities held by a bank or trust company, even though there is a fee for this service, because they believe such institutions are more reliable than brokerage firms.

Trustees and Executors

Trustees and executors handle property of a trust or an estate for the benefit of the people who share in it. A trustee or executor is required to follow state law and the terms of the document that created the trust, or the will of the person who left the estate, in disposing of the property. The principal responsibil-ities include collecting and distributing (or accumu-lating) the income of the trust or estate, buying and selling investments, and preparing accounting re-ports and tax returns.

An executor also is responsible for following the procedure provided by law to get property that is in the name of the person who died into the names of the people who share in the estate, after any debts and taxes due have been paid. This procedure, usu-ally referred to as "probate," often is expensive and lengthy.

In many parts of the country, fees for trustees and executors are either set by law or by generally fol-lowed custom in the community. For a trustee, an-nual fees may range from ½ percent to as much as 1 percent or more of the value of the trust property.

Often, a lower fee based on the value of the property is combined with a fee on income of the trust. An additional fee may be payable when money or property is distributed or when the trust ends.

Fees of executors usually combine a one time charge of a percentage of the value of estate assets handled by the executor with a percentage of income collected. This percentage of estate assets, combined with the fee of the lawyer for the estate, often amounts to between 5 and 10 percent of the value of the estate, depending on the estate's size and the amount of work required to handle it.

Sometimes it is possible to negotiate lower fees for a trustee or executor than those provided by law or the local fee schedule, if the fees would otherwise be unreasonably large in relation to the work involved. However, it often is not easy to conduct such negotiations effectively if a professional executor or trustee has already been named and therefore is legally entitled to act. A better negotiating position is likely to result if, rather than making an advance commitment as to who will be given the work, a family member or friend is named as trustee or executor and can then arrange for professional services to be performed as needed.

It is often suggested that expenses of administering your estate can be reduced by taking steps to "avoid probate" for the bulk of your property. Whether this would be true for you depends on local law and practice in regard to fees of executors and estate lawyers. A common way for individuals to avoid probate is by transferring property to a revocable trust, so that when they die it will not be in their name.* Your lawyer can advise you as to whether this procedure would make sense in your case.

Putting property in joint names, with a right of survivorship, is another technique for trying to avoid probate. However, it only works if the other joint owner in fact is the survivor. If you put property in joint names with someone who dies before you do, the property will then be yours alone, just as if you never had put it in joint names.

Financial-Planning Consultants

The newest professional group whose services are used in financial planning are commonly referred to as "financial-planning consultants" or "financial-planning advisers." Ideally, an individual or firm with that designation would undertake to review your entire financial situation and advise you on investments, insurance, and retirement arrangements, as well as your will and other aspects of the disposition of your property. It is obvious, though, that only an extraordinary individual could be well informed on all of these matters. There undoubtedly are some firms that do an excellent job by bringing the combined talents of top-flight professionals in each of the relevant fields to bear on clients' financial-planning problems, but they are hard to find.

Because the field is so new, few organizations have track records in providing this kind of general financial advice. The states have generally not undertaken to regulate professional practice in this

*See chapter 11, pp. 190–91.

area, aside from requiring investment advisers to register, so there is nothing to stop anyone from assuming the title of "financial-planning consultant" and obtaining a listing as such in the yellow pages of the telephone directory. To do so, it is not necessary to meet any specific educational requirements or to pass any examination.

The College of Financial Planning, an educational institution, does award people the title of "Certified Financial Planner." What this means is simply that an individual has taken some examinations, which can be prepared for through a home study course. Many people who have the title also are life insurance agents. Their advice to clients naturally may reflect their special familiarity with the life insurance they sell.

Indeed, a major problem for financial-planning consultants is to remain objective if part or all of their compensation comes from the sale of a particular product, such as life insurance, mutual funds, or tax shelters. The best way for consultants to achieve such objectivity is to be compensated specifically for services rendered—either through an hourly charge or a percentage of the value of the client's assets—rather than earning commissions by selling financial products.

If you want to find a financial-planning consultant, the best way to do so is to rely on the recommendation of another professional in whose judgment and objectivity you have complete confidence, and who does not stand to benefit either directly or indirectly if you employ a particular consultant.

Husbands (and Others)

Most states make it impossible for wives to completely disinherit their husbands (and vice versa). This means that a husband who survives his wife is legally entitled to a minimum share of her estate which cannot be taken away by her will, unless, through a marriage contract, he has effectively given up his right to claim the share. This right continues as long as the marriage is not terminated by divorce, even if the couple separates. The size of the husband's share may depend on whether the wife is also survived by children or other descendants. Often it is one-third. In some states, if there are no descendants, it is one-half.

The eight community property states—Arizona, California, Idaho, Louisiana, Nevada, New Mexico, Texas, and Washington—generally protect the surviving husband by giving him the absolute right to a half interest in the couple's community property,* but most give him no part of his wife's separate estate.

What happens if your marriage ends in divorce? In the community property states there will be a division of the community property. It is either fifty-fifty or the divorce court may make the division on some other basis, depending on the law of the particular state. In almost all of the other states, there also is a division of property. Many states, including some community property states, allow the divorce court to divide everything owned by either the husband

*See chapter 4, pp. 78–81, for a discussion of community property.

or the wife. Other states limit the division to certain property acquired during marriage.

If you have a family from a previous marriage and are considering marrying again, you may be worried about the effect that your remarriage may have on your children's and grandchildren's shares in your estate. Women (and men) in this situation sometimes attempt to use an "antenuptual agreement," or marriage contract. Such contracts are quite common in some foreign countries but are still sufficiently unusual here to be a sensitive subject for people who are considering marriage, particularly a first marriage. The contract usually seeks to limit the rights of the husband or the wife or of both to be assigned property of the other spouse in the event of divorce or to inherit property from the other spouse. Rights of inheritance and on divorce are given by state law, and states vary in their willingness to enforce contracts that seek to limit those rights. The results often depend on the facts of the particular case.

You may, of course, sign a marriage contract and get married in one state and then later move to another state. In such a case your husband's rights may be determined by the law of the second state, which may be different from the law of the state where you were married. Whether you can rely on a marriage contract is something for you to discuss with your lawyer.

Another alternative, which is not effective in most states but may work in a few places, is for you to transfer your property to a revocable trust. Occasionally, a state does not allow a husband to claim a minimum share of property in a revocable trust created by his wife, even though he could claim such a share of property disposed of by her will.

The marriage of your child can also affect your planning. If you plan to make a substantial gift to your son or daughter, you should keep in mind that part of the property you are giving could end up with an ex-daughter-in-law or ex-son-in-law if your son or daughter marries and the marriage ends in divorce. Even if the judge who grants the divorce is not authorized by state law to take property that was given to one spouse and assign it to the other spouse, he or she may take it into account in setting the amount of alimony to be paid.

Admittedly, the risk that property given to a son may end up with his ex-wife is far greater today than the risk that property given to a daughter will end up with her ex-husband. Judges are more likely to assign a husband's property to his ex-wife on divorce, or to order him to pay alimony to her, than vice versa. However, the Supreme Court has held that a state may not provide alimony only for wives and not for husbands. Also, with improved career opportunities for women, there are a growing number of cases in which the wife supports the family to a greater extent than the husband. Thus, the risk that property given to a daughter may be assigned to her ex-husband or taken to pay alimony to him may increase as the law continues to move in the direction of more equal treatment of the sexes.

An important way to minimize these kinds of risks is for you to give the property in trust for your son or daughter, instead of directly to him or her. If the property is not owned by your child at the time of the divorce, the judge will be unable to assign it to the ex-in-law (although, of course, it may still be considered in fixing alimony).

What has been said about husbands and in-laws sometimes may apply to couples who live together without being married. The best-known example of a claim based on such a relationship was Michelle Triola's suit against Lee Marvin, in which she claimed a one-half interest in his earnings during the period of time the couple had lived together, even though they were never married. Although she ultimately did not succeed in collecting anything from Marvin, he was forced to incur substantial legal expenses—over $250,000 by one estimate—to defend his position.

Similar suits by others have sometimes been successful. As a result, couples who plan to live together sometimes execute "anti-Marvin" or "cohabitation" agreements, which seek to define and limit their rights to each other's property. As this is a developing area of law, the legal effectiveness of such agreements is unsettled.

The American Bar Association has published a useful booklet, "Law and Marriage," dealing with the legal rights and duties of both married couples and couples living together. It can be ordered for $1 per copy, plus $1 for handling each order, from the American Bar Association, Order Fulfillment, 1155 East 60th Street, Chicago, IL 60637.

PART II

HOW TO HANDLE
YOUR PROPERTY

WHEN YOU *acquire property you must decide in whose name to put it. Should your property be held in your name alone, in joint names with your husband or someone else, or in community with your husband (if you live in a community property state)? These alternatives are compared in chapter 4 of this part.*

If you hold property as an investment, rather than for personal use, you also need to decide when it should be sold and the proceeds invested in something else. More active management is needed for some investments, such as real estate that is leased to tenants and may require arrangements for repairs and upkeep, as well as payment of taxes and insurance.

Too often these decisions are made without sufficient thought. When you decide how to hold title to your property or how to invest your money, you are making some of the most important financial deci-

sions you will ever make—decisions that can determine whether you and those you want to help have a comfortable amount to live on.

If you have money to invest, you have a choice as to whether you should own stocks, bonds, mutual fund shares, money market funds, real estate, life insurance, savings accounts, money market bank accounts, bank certificates of deposit, or other kinds of investments. You also have a choice as to who should manage your investments, if you decide not to do the job yourself. These choices are discussed in chapter 5.

An important aspect of managing your property is protecting your rights if you have an interest in an estate or in a trust created by someone else. Chapter 6 discusses steps you can take to be sure that you receive all that you have coming to you.

CHAPTER 4

Whose Name to Put Your Property In

WHETHER to hold property in your name alone or jointly with someone else is an important choice. For women who have enough property to be seriously concerned with estate and gift taxes, the decision becomes somewhat complicated as well. So this chapter deals only with choices for women for whom these taxes are not a serious concern.*

The available choices in holding your property are determined by the law of your state and usually include most or all of the following:

1. In your name alone: Margaret Rhodes
2. As tenants in common: Margaret Rhodes and Peter Harrison as tenants in common

---

*Ways to save gift taxes are discussed in chapter 14 and ways to save estate taxes in chapter 15.

3. As joint tenants: Margaret Rhodes and Peter Harrison as joint tenants with right of survivorship and not as tenants in common

Married women may have two other options as well:

4. As tenants by the entirety: Jennie Stevens and Don Stevens as tenants by the entirety
5. In community with your husband (if you live in a community property state—Arizona, California, Idaho, Louisiana, New Mexico, Nevada, Texas, and Washington)

Your Name Alone

Holding property in your name alone is often the simplest alternative, but it can involve complications. Upon your death, some legal procedure will be required to move the property from your name into the names of the people named in your will, or your heirs if you die without a will. If the property is a security or a bank account, this will be accomplished by probate of your estate. The executor named in your will will follow the procedures provided by state law to pay your debts and taxes and to turn over what is left to whoever is entitled to it. If you leave no will, or the person you name as executor does not carry out the job, the court will appoint an administrator to act instead.

If the property is real estate, the states are divided

as to whether the title passes first to your executor and then to the people who will share your estate or whether it passes directly to them without your executor being involved at all. In either case, however, the property may be sold if money is needed to pay your debts.

Tenants In Common

In many states, if property is transferred to two or more people who are not husband and wife,* it is assumed that they will be tenants in common if nothing to the contrary is written in the deed. For example, if Margaret Rhodes and her friend Peter Harrison put up equal amounts of money to buy a house and the deed reads simply "Margaret Rhodes and Peter Harrison," they are usually held to be tenants in common. This means that each of them has a half interest in the property. If Margaret had put up two-thirds of the money and Peter only one-third, a court might find that they intended her to have a two-thirds interest and for Peter to have a one-third interest. In either case, each of them has the right to live in the house.

What happens if they don't get along or if one wants to sell the house and the other doesn't? Either of them can ask the court to order a sale and division

---

*In some states, a husband and wife are assumed to hold property as tenants by the entirety.

of the proceeds. This means that the property is sold at auction. Either of them may buy the house at the auction sale and become sole owner of it. The proceeds of the sale are divided between them in proportion to their interests in the house, after deduction of the selling expenses.

If Margaret died while she and Peter each held a half interest in the property as tenants in common, her one-half interest would be disposed of under her will, or if she left no will, her one-half interest would go to her heirs as determined by the law of the state in which the house was located. She may prefer that her interest go to Peter instead.

Tenancy in common is a widely used form of ownership for people who are not married to each other. For example, if Mary Smith died without a will and two daughters survived her, Mary's house would pass to them as tenants in common. It is another way to have property in your own name. The only difference is that in a tenancy in common, what is in your name is a fractional interest in property, rather than the entire property.

Joint Tenancy

If Margaret and Peter own their house as joint tenants with right of survivorship, then, as with a tenancy in common, each of them has an interest in the property and the right to live in the house. If they can't get along, they can agree to sell the property and divide the sale proceeds, and if they can't agree on a sale, either of them can ask the court to order the property sold. Either of them can dispose of his or her interest at any time.

One important difference between joint tenancy and tenancy in common is that if one of the joint tenants dies, the other owns the entire property. No part of it passes under the will of the one who died, or to his or her heirs. If a joint tenant wants to avoid this, then he or she should take steps to end the joint tenancy, either by having the property sold and dividing the proceeds or by converting it into a tenancy in common.

If the joint tenancy is in a bank account or brokerage account, depending on state law it may be possible for either joint tenant to withdraw money or property from the account. This could mean that a woman who opened such an account could lose what she put into it, if the other joint tenant made withdrawals.

For women who have enough wealth to be concerned about estate taxes, joint tenancy may be a costly way to hold title to property.* Married women who hold property in joint tenancy with their husbands do not have the same reasons to be concerned about estate taxes, but may find that the arrangement is expensive from an income tax standpoint.†

*See chapter 15, pp. 237–38.
†See chapter 13, pp. 210–11.

Tenancy by the Entirety

Fewer than half the states recognize tenancy by the entirety, a form of joint ownership limited to married couples. In some of those states, it is very much like joint tenancy with survivorship, and the husband or the wife can dispose of his or her interest at any time. In a few states, it may still be impossible for either spouse to dispose of his or her interest without the consent of the other, as long as both are living. When either of them dies, it belongs to the other.

As tenancy by the entirety is limited to married couples, it ends on divorce. Either the divorce court will award the property to one of the spouses, or, if the court does not make such an award, the divorce decree may automatically change the property into a tenancy in common.

As with joint tenancy, married women who hold property in tenancy by the entirety with their husbands may find the arrangement is expensive from an income tax standpoint.*

In Community

In eight states—Arizona, California, Idaho, Louisiana, Nevada, New Mexico, Texas, and Washington—married people usually hold title to most of the property

* See chapter 13, pp. 210–11.

they acquire during marriage "in community." Exactly what property is treated this way, and what the effects are, depends on the laws of the particular state.

The basic idea behind the community property laws is to treat marriage as a partnership and the property acquired during the marriage, with certain exceptions, as belonging to husband and wife in equal shares. Property owned at the time of the marriage and property acquired during the marriage by gift or under a will or by inheritance is not treated as community property. Instead, it is the separate property of the spouse who acquires it, unless it becomes commingled with community property and loses its identity as separate property because its source cannot be proved.

In Texas, Louisiana, and Idaho, the income during marriage from separate property belongs to the husband and wife in community. In the other community property states, such income from separate property is also separate property. For example, if Louise owns stock that she bought before she married, the dividends she receives after she marries are her separate property unless she lives in one of the three states that treat income from separate property as community property.

Community property often is confusing to people who did not grow up in one of the eight community property states—and even to some who have lived there all of their lives. In those states, a deed to real estate or a stock certificate may be in the name of only one spouse and may not show that the real estate or stock is community property. The rules of the particular state may nevertheless treat it as such. It is easier to establish that a particular item is your separate property if there is a written record that you hold it as your "sole and separate property."

One important result of treating property as community property is that when either the husband or the wife dies, he or she can dispose of half of the community property by his or her will. If the marriage ends in divorce, the community property is divided. In some states it is always a fifty-fifty split, and in others the divorce court may use some discretion in making the division.

Can you or your husband make a gift of community property during your life, without the consent of the other spouse? This is a complicated question, and the answer may depend on which state you live in. Complications also arise when both separate and community property are used to pay for a particular item. For example, some life insurance premiums may be paid with your husband's separate property, some with yours, and some with community property. When your husband dies, what happens to the proceeds? The states have different ways of working this out.

In most of the community property states, husbands and wives can agree to ignore the community property laws and hold whatever property they acquire separately from each other. Such agreements are unusual, however, and should be made only with a lawyer's advice.

Suppose you and your husband move from a state like New York, which does not have community property, to a state like California, which does. Does this change the property you acquired while you were living in New York into community property? For purposes of division on divorce or death, California will treat some of the property you acquired back east as if it were community property. For example, suppose you earned and saved $50,000 while you were married and living in New York and invested it in stock. If you and your husband move to California and you die or are divorced there, one-half of the stock belongs to your husband as "quasi-community property." Not all the community property states treat property acquired in another state the same way California does.

Suppose your move is in the other direction. You live in California at the time of your marriage, and you put $50,000 of your earnings into stock. You then move to New York. Will New York follow California law and treat the stock as community property for purposes of division on divorce or death? In New York the answer is clearly yes, but in other non-community-property states the rule is not always as clear.

CHAPTER 5

Managing Your Investments

WHEN my father died thirty-three years ago, I lost my first—and best—investment manager. He made his mistakes in handling my savings, but the results of his management were generally good. He charged no fees, and I knew that he always had my interests at heart. This gave me peace of mind, which I later found I valued more than the greater profits sometimes made at the cost of great anxiety about investments.

If you have a manager who combines these characteristics, you can skip this chapter. It cannot point the way to a more satisfactory arrangement for your investments than the one you have now.

What can you do if you do not have such a paragon to rely on? The following are your major alternatives:

1. Being your own manager
2. Relying on your broker
3. Employing an investment manager
4. Owning shares in mutual funds and holding bank accounts and certificates of deposit

Before you make this choice, you should decide how much risk you are willing to assume when you invest.

It was formerly common to emphasize also that you should decide whether you were more interested in current income or in having your investments go up in value. This distinction has become less important in recent years, as investors have paid more attention to their total return from investments in interest or dividends and growth in value, rather than just the part that is income. Nevertheless, if you depend on the income from your investments to cover your living expenses, you may find it hard to spend any part of your principal, even though it has gone up in value by more than the amount that you are spending even after allowing for inflation. If this is true for you, income, rather than total return, is an important factor to take into account.

If your top income tax bracket is as much as 30 or 35 percent, the form in which you receive your income makes a big difference in the taxes you pay. You will want to receive as much of the total return on your investments as possible in a form that will be subject to little or no income tax. For example, you may want to buy bonds that are tax-exempt, rather than bonds on which the interest is fully taxable, even though the tax-exempt bonds pay a lower rate of interest. However, you should also consider carefully the disadvantages of owning tax-exempt bonds—disadvantages that are shared with many bonds that are fully taxable:

1. When interest rates are going up, bond prices may fall sharply;
2. Even though interest rates have not gone up, there is likely to be a substantial discount if you want to sell fewer than $25,000 bonds of a single issue before maturity;
3. The amount of principal and interest you will receive is fixed in "frozen dollars," rather than being adjusted for inflation;
4. There could be a default in payment of principal or interest, although generally the record of tax-exempt bonds in this respect is good.

Instead of buying tax-exempt bonds directly, you may buy shares in a mutual fund which invests in such bonds.

You also may want to buy stocks that pay relatively low dividends but which you believe can be expected to grow in value. If you sell your shares in order to realize the income which that growth represents, any gain on the sale will be taxed as capital gain, rather than as ordinary income. This means that if you hold the stock for more than one year before you sell it, only 40 percent of your gain is taxable.

If you do not sell the stock during your lifetime, whoever receives it after your death will have a new cost to use in figuring gain or loss, based on the value at the time of your death. No income taxes will have to be paid on the increase in value during your life. Again, however, there is a possible disadvantage in buying growth stocks to save taxes: If the business fails to grow, the price of the stock may drop sharply.

Risk of Loss

Before you choose a manager for your investments, you should decide how much risk of loss you are willing to accept. Investments range in riskiness from practically risk-free short-term United States Treasury obligations to commodity futures contracts and other speculative investments which carry a very high risk of loss. Willingness and ability to risk losing what you have in the hope of making more depends very much on your financial situation and temperament. For example, if Mary, an elderly widow, is concerned with covering her living expenses, she is in no position to put her savings in any investment that is very risky. Louise, on the other hand, who has a million dollars plus the income from a $600,000 trust fund, is probably in a position to take some chances with her money if she wishes to do so in the hope getting a larger return.

Any generalization about which investments are more or less risky involves predictions that are difficult to make. At times, even long-term United States Government bonds have declined substantially in price because the interest rate payable on the bonds was below that currently prevailing for new bond issues. And companies that are highly regarded may suffer losses and even go into bankruptcy. But some people simply do not use good judgment in taking risks, even in light of the facts that are known when the investment is made.

Two examples of poor judgment about risks stick in my mind. The first involves a widow who was persuaded to sell her United States Government bonds and put all of her life savings into higher yielding but riskier bonds of South American governments. The South American bonds promptly stopped paying any interest. As a result, she had to support herself and her son by renting rooms and taking a secretarial job. At the other extreme, a wealthy widow I knew insisted on keeping $100,000 in her non-interest-bearing checking account at all times so that she would not feel poor, even though her wealth amounted to several million dollars.

After you have decided how much risk you are prepared to assume, you can choose the alternative for management of your investments that suits your temperament, needs, interests, and financial situation.

Investment Management Alternatives

Being Your Own Manager

Many people decide to rely on themselves for investment management. Whether this will be a satisfactory arrangement for you depends on whether you combine the temperament, knowledge, and willingness to spend time on investments that your particular method of investing requires. For example, a woman I know who I'll call Sarah bought stocks in major corporations at what hindsight tells us was a good time to buy—the mid-1940s. Most of Sarah's holdings have done well for her. She has not been particularly concerned about fluctuations in the prices of her stocks, because she treats them as long-range investments and does not try to sell when prices are high or to buy more when prices are low. When she has additional savings to invest, she uses bank certificates of deposit, money market bank accounts, and money market mutual funds.

Sarah's investment strategy has worked well for her because she chose a favorable time to invest and because following her investments does not require more time than she is willing to commit. Her strategy suits her calm temperament and her confidence that the major corporations she has invested in will survive and prosper.

If Sarah's strategy appeals to you and you have money to invest, you still have the problem of determining when the time is right to buy stocks—or, if you prefer, bonds. With hindsight, that looks easy. We now know that the spring of 1982 was an ideal time to buy almost any kind of security, but that was not as clear then. However, whether or not you manage to buy your investments at a favorable time, you have the option of following Sarah's approach and ignoring changes in market prices. Of course you can, if you wish, make no effort to choose the "right" time to buy—something which even the experts have trouble doing consistently. If this strategy suits you, it is relatively easy for you to be your own investment manager.

At the opposite end of the spectrum from Sarah is a woman I'll call Marie, a widow with a large number of securities which she follows on a daily basis. For her, investments are a hobby as well as her main source of income. She spends many hours every week reading financial journals and sometimes sits at her broker's watching the ticker tape that reports trading in stocks. She often discusses stocks with her broker, but in the end, she makes her own decisions.

Instead of viewing her stocks as long-range investments in businesses, Marie is more of a trader. She looks upon her securities the way a retail merchant looks at his inventory and constantly tries to buy undiscovered stocks that will later come into favor with other investors.

Marie has had her good years and her bad years with investments. It is difficult for her to insulate herself from the prevailing climate of opinion among investors. As a result, she sometimes finds that she has been swept along with a strong tide of sentiment and has sold near the bottom or bought near the top. Her children wish she would take up a less demanding hobby and turn over investing to someone else, but she prefers to go on being her own manager.

Marie's strategy requires much more time than Sarah's but has the possibility of producing far greater profits if you are successful in carrying it out. However, few people manage to follow Marie's strategy successfully over any extended period. In order to do so, they must be right about the market often enough to more than make up for the added taxes and brokerage commissions that must be paid. And some people find that Marie's approach generates so much anxiety for them that it is not worth the potential profits.

There are, of course, many points in between Sarah's buy-and-hold strategy and Marie's trading. You should decide what suits you best and whether, on balance, you prefer to be your own manager or to turn the job over to someone else.

Relying On Your Broker

A great many women rely on their brokers for advice and some undoubtedly get excellent investment results from this source. However, as I have already pointed out, the fact that brokers earn their living by executing orders to buy or sell securities makes it very difficult for them to recommend that you do nothing, even when this would be the best course. It is sometimes said that optimism is the vice of brokers. Many find it hard to tell customers to sell any stock except to buy another stock.

If you can find a broker whose services are satisfactory and whose advice you are willing to rely on, it will take less of your time than being your own manager (unless you adopt Sarah's buy-and-hold strategy). It also will save the fees you would have to pay if you hired an investment manager.

Relying On an Investment Manager

Investment managers (often called investment counsel) undertake either to advise you about investments or to act on your behalf in making purchases and sales through brokers. The second arrangement, in which you give the manager discretion to act for you, is more common because it saves time by eliminating the need for consultations before buying or selling. Some women doubtless have gotten excellent advice from these sources. But as a practical matter, only women with substantial securities portfolios have access to the advice of most investment managers. It is not unusual to find that the minimum size account a firm will accept is $250,000 or even $500,000. Some firms start much higher and restrict themselves to accounts of several millions.

There are investment counsel that accept smaller accounts. But the fees are likely to be relatively high because of the cost of handling a large number of small accounts. And given the number of firms that refuse to accept small accounts, it can be difficult to find top-notch counsel for them.

Ownership of Mutual Funds

Mutual fund shares are an ideal investment medium for many people. Mutual funds are organized as corporations or trusts in accordance with state law for the purpose of investing in securities of other corporations or governmental bodies. If you buy shares in a mutual fund, your money is pooled with the funds provided by other buyers of shares and the total amount is invested under the supervision of investment counsel. This arrangement allows relatively small amounts—many mutual funds will accept initial investments of as little as $250—to be combined for investment purposes into sums large enough to be invested in a large number of different securities, managed by investment professionals. Many people believe that dividing a fund for investment among a number of different securities instead of putting all of the nest eggs in a single basket reduces the risk of major losses.

Of course, neither diversifying investments nor professional management is any guarantee against loss, and there are mutual funds whose investment results have been highly disappointing. But for women who do not want to manage their investments themselves and do not have enough money to employ individual investment counsel, a professionally managed mutual fund is likely to be more satisfactory than relying on a broker's advice. At least it should reduce the time spent on and anxiety produced by investing.

For women who want to play a more active part in managing their investments, mutual funds may be used in other ways. Many sponsoring organizations offer a number of different mutual funds with a variety of investment policies and objectives. For example, the sponsor may have a growth stock fund, an income-oriented stock fund, and a money market fund which invests in short-term notes of corporations or governments and bank certificates of deposit. There may even be specialized funds, investing only in securities of companies in a particular kind of business. It is common practice to allow mutual fund shareholders to switch between different funds of the same sponsoring organization, often by telephone. This allows an investor to sell shares in one fund and buy shares in another quickly, without incurring any expense.

In addition to providing investment management, ownership of shares in mutual funds often may be used to meet the needs of an investor for custody and tax records as well. This is because the funds offer to keep custody of certificates for shares, and the accounting statements contain the necessary information for tax returns.

Mutual funds may be either "open end" or "closed end." Open-end funds are more common, and offer shares directly to investors, either with or without a sales charge. These funds also generally will redeem shares from investors who want to sell at the net asset value at the time of redemption (which may be more or less than the purchase price). Closed-end funds do not regularly buy or sell their own shares, so that you must buy from another shareholder instead of from the fund itself. So there are three alternatives generally available:

1. *No-load open-end funds.* These funds have no salesman and you pay no commission to buy the shares. You send in an application and check to the fund yourself. What you pay is the "net asset value" of the shares, which means the total value of the fund's investments divided by the number of its shares that are outstanding. For example, if the fund's investments are worth $10 million and it has 1 million shares outstanding, the net asset value per share would be $10. If you bought 100 shares, the cost would be $1,000.

2. *Load open-end funds.* These funds pay commissions to brokers who sell the fund's shares, and you are

charged a commission when you buy. What you pay is the "net asset value" of the shares plus a sales charge, typically 8½ percent. This means that if you buy 100 shares with a net asset value of $10 per share, you will pay $1,085. There are also a few "low-load" funds, for which the sales charge may be as low as 2 or 3 percent.

In my opinion, there is *no* reason ever to buy shares in regular load funds. No-load and low-load funds can be equally desirable investments and yet do not require the 8½ percent commission. The same is true of publicly traded closed-end fund shares if they are not selling at a premium over net asset value. Of course, either a no-load or closed-end fund may be less attractive if it has high expenses, which are deducted either from current earnings or from assets of the fund.

3. *Closed-end funds.* These funds are investment companies whose stock often is listed on a stock exchange. Their shares have frequently sold at a discount. This means that if the fund's investments are worth $10 million and it has one million shares outstanding, even though the net asset value is $10 per share the market price may be only $8 or $9 per share. One reason for this difference is that closed-end funds do not undertake to redeem shares from investors who want to sell. An investor who wants to sell must do so through a broker, paying a commission. The price will be determined by what a buyer is willing to pay, rather than by the value of the securities owned by the fund.

Bear in mind that all funds pay a fee to an investment manager and incur expenses which will reduce the return on your investment in the fund. Before choosing one, you should carefully review the prospectus which all funds are required to have and which describes in detail the fund's objectives and methods of operation.

Money market mutual funds are in a class by themselves because they serve many of the purposes of checking accounts. By valuing their investments at cost, these funds generally are able to maintain a fixed price for their shares, usually $1.

When banks were more severely restricted by law as to the interest they could pay on checking accounts, money market funds served an important purpose for investors, by allowing small investors to earn high yields on short-term investments. Banks have been partially freed from these restrictions and can pay higher interest than before on certain kinds of checking accounts. Many banks and savings and loan associations now offer money market accounts that pay interest at fluctuating rates that are competitive with money market mutual funds. Most of these accounts have the advantage over a mutual fund of being federally insured to the same extent as a bank checking account.

On the other hand, money market accounts, under federal regulations, require varying minimum balances and may limit the number of checks (other than checks you cash yourself at the bank) that can be written on the account each month. If you violate these account restrictions, interest penalties will apply and the higher yield of the money market account will be lost. You should take these restrictions into account in determining whether your needs would best be met by a money market mutual fund or a money market bank or savings and loan account, or a combination of both. However, check limits can easily be avoided if you have another checking account in the same place and make transfers to it as needed from your money market account.

Another alternative is bank certificates of deposit, if you wish to earn a fixed interest rate on your funds for a specified period of time and are willing to forego withdrawing the money in the meantime.

An informative biweekly guide to mutual fund shares is the "United Mutual Fund Selector." Subscriptions may be ordered from 210 Newbury Street, Boston, Massachusetts 02116, at the cost of $75 a year. Another source of information about mutual funds is Weisenberger's "Investment Companies," a more expensive publication giving more data. It may be available at your local library.

CHAPTER 6

How to Protect Your Rights in an Estate or Trust

IF you are entitled to money or property from the estate of someone who has died, or from a trust created by someone other than you, it is important to be sure that you get what you are entitled to without paying unnecessary legal fees to enforce your rights. Those rights, and the procedures followed in dealing with them, are substantially different for estates, discussed in the first section of the chapter, and for trusts, discussed in the second section.

Protecting Your Rights in an Estate

You may be entitled to money or property from an estate, either because you are named in the will or as an heir under the state intestacy statute, if the person who died left no will. In this situation, the executor or administrator who handles the estate is under a legal duty to act fairly and impartially to protect your interest, as well as the interests of other people who share under the will or as heirs. If you have confidence that the executor is carrying out this duty, asking a lawyer about your rights may result in your paying legal fees for services you don't need. However, you should get a copy of the will and have a general idea of what your rights are, as well as of the procedures that will be followed in settling the estate.

The situation is different if the person died with a will that may not be legally effective to dispose of all of his or her property, either because it was incomplete or because it was invalid. A will is invalid if it was made by someone who did not have the mental capacity required by state law to make a valid will, or if it was executed as a result of fraud, duress, or undue influence, or without the required formalities. If you would be entitled to a share as an heir under the state intestacy statute had there been no will, and if the will is subject to attack on any of these grounds, you should consult a lawyer promptly about your rights and the way to enforce them. *You cannot rely on the executor to do this for you.* The executor's duty is to uphold the will and not to find grounds for declaring it invalid.

If you are the widow, you usually are entitled under state law to claim a share of the estate without regard to the provisions of the will. Again, the executor's duty is to act for the people named in the will, rather than for you. If you wish to assert your right to a share rather than accepting the provisions of the will, you should consult a lawyer promptly about your rights and the way to enforce them.

You may be interested in an estate because you have a claim for money or property due to you from the person who died. For example, you may have loaned money to him or her, or the title to property that belongs to you may have been in his or her name. If a large amount is involved, you should consult your lawyer promptly about how to protect your rights. The time provided by law for you to file your claim against an estate usually is short. If you fail to file your claim within that time, the executor will be legally unable to pay your claim even though he or she may wish to do so.

You may feel that you know an individual executor well enough to rely on him or her to help you take the necessary legal steps to have your claim paid, even though there is no legal duty to look out for your interests. But if the executor dies or resigns before those steps have been taken, the successor may not be as willing to help.

Procedures for settling estates vary greatly from state to state in matters of detail, but usually follow a basic pattern. The person named in the will to act as executor petitions the court to be appointed. If no one objects and the executor is not disqualified for some reason, the appointment will be made and the executor can then begin to act. Before acting as such, the executor may be required to give bond for the protection of people who are interested in the estate.

The bond provides a form of insurance, so that if the executor goes off with the assets of the estate, the bonding company undertakes to replace them. But the cost of that insurance is a high premium, which must be paid for by the estate. So it is common for the will to provide that no bond shall be required, in order to save this expense. Many people feel that if the person making the will believes that the executor should be bonded, it would have been better to have named someone else instead.

The first major duty of the executor is to take possession of the property of the person who died. Usually the executor must prepare and file an inventory in the probate court, giving the value of the property. If the property consists of securities that are quoted in the newspaper, or bank accounts or other kinds of property whose value can be easily figured, making the inventory may be relatively simple. But if the person who died owned real estate, stock in a closely held corporation whose shares are not traded on the stock exchange or in the national over-the-counter market, works of art, or other items of unusual value, then the process becomes more difficult. Depending on the amount involved, the executor may employ expert appraisers to value particular kinds of property.

If you are the widow or an heir or legatee named in the will, you are entitled to a copy of the inventory of the estate, as well as the will. If the executor does not send them, request that he or she do so.

After the inventory has been filed, the administration of the estate may follow either of two basic patterns. Under a court-supervised administration, the executor must obtain approval of the probate court for a great many of the actions involved in handling the estate—such as selling estate property, paying claims against the estate, and paying money or turning over property to people who have shares in the estate. Many states now permit the will to give the executor the power to act without such court supervision. If the executor has been given such power, court approval may not be needed until the point at which the executor files an account of his or her administration and a plan to turn over the money and property remaining on hand to the people who are entitled to receive it.

Many states require an executor to file accounts in court telling how he or she has handled the property and money of the estate. In other states, filing such an account is voluntary, but an executor may choose to file it anyway in order to get a court to determine that the legal duties have been carried out. The executor is responsible for paying valid claims, taxes, legacies, and expenses of administration, and then turning over whatever remains to the people who are entitled to receive it. In order to make these payments, it will often be necessary to sell assets of the estate. If the selling price is either more or less than the value given in the inventory, that difference will be reflected as a gain or loss in the executor's account. There may be a "first and final account," covering all receipts and payments during administration of the estate, or if the administration is long-drawn-out and complicated, accounts may be made on an annual basis.

You may be asked to approve the executor's account of the amounts received and payments made before it is filed in court for approval by the judge. If this occurs, be sure you are satisfied that the payments for which the executor claims credit were proper and that the estate's property was handled with reasonable care. When you approve an account, you are giving up your right to object to what the executor did and to claim that he or she is liable to the estate for damage it suffered from his or her acts. This includes not merely the sale of estate property but also the failure to make sales when it would have made sense to do so. However, you should not assume that merely because property held by the estate, such as stock, declined in value, the executor was under a duty to sell it to avoid loss to the estate. An executor is expected to act with reasonably good judgment, not to make no mistakes.

People who are not themselves lawyers find it difficult to understand why the administration of an estate may drag on for three or four years, or even longer, particularly if there are no disputes among the people who have shares in the estate. In recent years efforts have been made to shorten the period of administration and to simplify the procedure. Nevertheless, the process still may take a long time, particularly if the estate is large enough to require a federal estate tax return to be filed. At present, a return is required if the value of the estate (before deductions) is over $325,000, but that amount will increase each year until it reaches $600,000 for people dying in 1987 or later.

The federal estate tax is not due until nine months after a person dies. Usually, it is unwise to file the return and pay the tax more than a few days early for two reasons. First, the executor has the choice of valuing the estate either as of the date of death or on the "alternate valuation date"—generally six months later. Before comparing the total value of the property in the estate on each of these two dates, the executor cannot know which date is better to use. Second, if the tax is paid early, the estate loses interest that could have been earned on the money used to pay the tax.

After the return is filed, it is likely to be audited by the Internal Revenue Service to determine whether the correct amount of tax has been paid. Depending on the backlog of work for the estate examiners in a particular district, the audit may not be finished for a year or more after the return is filed. When it is complete, the Internal Revenue Service may decide that the estate tax return should be accepted as filed. But often it will find that additional items should be included or the values of items reported should be increased. If the executor does not agree with these findings, there will be further delays while the differences are resolved. If they cannot be resolved informally, court action will be required. Each step can take several months.

After any disagreements between the executor and the Internal Revenue Service have been settled, the executor can then deal with the state tax authorities. Many states impose an inheritance tax, based on the size of each person's share in the estate, in addition to an estate tax, based on the size of the entire estate.

Although most estates are not large enough to require the filing of a federal estate tax return, the minimum amount to file a state inheritance or estate tax return is often considerably lower. Moreover, where a federal return is required, the state tax authorities are unwilling to determine the amount due them until the Internal Revenue Service has made its final determination. So state tax problems may cause delays even if there are none caused by the federal requirements.

In addition to estate and inheritance tax returns, the executor must file a final income tax return for the person who died, reporting income up to the date of his or her death, as well as income tax returns for the estate itself for whatever period of time is required to settle it. If there are disputes over the amount of income taxes due, there may be further delay in settling the estate.

Another source of delay may be the backlog of work in the office of the lawyer who is handling the estate. Busy lawyers can't do everything at once, and settling an estate may take a back seat when they are pressed with deadlines in court cases that cannot be extended readily. If the attorney for the estate you are interested in seems to be in this position, it is a question of judgment whether prodding from you will help speed things up rather than merely making him or her angry.

The fees of executors and their attorneys are often

a source of dismay to people who share in an estate. It is only a partial consolation when they learn that the fees may be deducted for estate tax purposes or from the income of the estate for income tax purposes, whichever saves more taxes. Fees generally are based on a sliding scale percentage of the value of the estate, with various adjustments. The percentage declines as the amount involved increases. This fee schedule either may be provided by state law or may merely represent the practice of professional executors and their attorneys in the particular locality.

In New York, for example, the statutory sliding scale for executors ranges from 5 percent on the first $100,000 to 2 percent on the excess over $5 million. If there are two executors, each gets a full fee at these rates (unless one of them is a family member or friend who waives the right to a fee). Moreover, some New York City banks will not serve as executor for less than a minimum fee of $15,000.

Fees vary widely among states and even among different executors and attorneys within a single state. It is not unknown for executors and attorneys to agree to accept a reduced fee if the estate is large and the amount of work does not justify a fee based on the usual percentages.

When you receive money or property from an estate, it may or may not be subject to income tax. This is because legacies (gifts of personal property by will) are not included in income for tax purposes unless they are considered to represent income earned by the estate. A legacy of a specific sum of money or of specific property is generally not considered to represent income for tax purposes. For example, if your aunt leaves you $25,000 in her will, when you receive the money from her executor you will not have to treat any of it as taxable income.

A gift of a share of the property that remains after debts, taxes, and legacies have been paid, on the other hand, is regarded as including a share of income earned by the estate. For example, suppose your husband leaves you his entire estate. If the executor transfers stock worth $25,000 to you as part of this bequest in a year when the estate has income of $10,000, part of the stock you receive will be regarded as representing that much income of the estate. The estate will be entitled to a deduction of $10,000 on account of the stock that was distributed to you. You will be required to include that amount in your income for tax purposes.

If the residue goes to two people, each includes a share of estate income each year in proportion to the distributions he or she received from the estate in that year. Suppose your husband had left you half of his estate and the other half to your daughter and you each received a distribution of stock worth $25,000. The estate would get the same total deduction for the distributions, $10,000, and you and your daughter would each include $5,000 in income as a result.

The executor should give you information as to what part of what you receive from an estate should be included in your income for tax purposes. If you receive property from an estate, such as securities, the executor should tell you what to treat as your cost for tax purposes in figuring your gain or loss if you sell.

Protecting Your Rights in a Trust

If you have a share of a trust, your position is similar in many ways to that of someone who has a share of an estate. Like the executor of an estate, a trustee is under a legal duty to act fairly and impartially to protect your interest, as well as the interests of other people who have shares in the trust. As with an executor, if you have confidence that the trustee is carrying out this duty, there is probably no need to consult a lawyer, but you should be informed. That is, you should have a copy of the document creating the trust, and you should know in a general way what your rights are and what procedures should be followed in handling the trust.

You should also make a regular practice of discussing with the trustee any questions that you may have about the trust. Many professional trustees do not keep in close touch with trust beneficiaries and may not know, for example, that you need additional amounts of income or principal in order to meet your expenses.

There are two basic differences in the position of people who share in trusts and estates. First, trusts are likely to last a great deal longer than estates, even though it can take a relatively long time to settle estates. It is very unusual for an estate to take more than five years to be settled; one or two years is common. Some trusts may last for as long as eighty or even one hundred years. As a result, distributions of trust property are likely to be in smaller amounts over a longer period of time, instead of a few lump sums. Second, trustees are far more likely than executors to be given the power to determine whether or not money should be paid to a given beneficiary.

Procedures for handling trusts vary greatly in matters of detail, but as with estates usually follow basic patterns depending on whether or not the trust is supervised by a court. If it is a court trust, the trustee named in the will must also be appointed by a probate court and must file accounts with the court periodically, reporting all amounts received and payments made. This may be expensive, if guardians must be appointed to check over the accounts in order to protect the interests of people who cannot legally do so for themselves, such as minors. It also means that the accounts are open to the public. Anyone can go to the courthouse and find out how much property is in the trust and how much income has been paid out to each person.

In most states a trust set up by someone during his or her lifetime is a "noncourt" trust. This means that the trustees do not have to be appointed by a court and do not have to file accounts in court unless their handling of the trust is questioned by someone who has a share in it.

Whether a trust is a court or noncourt trust, the trustee's duties include the preparation of accounts which set forth the way the property and money of the trust has been handled. These accounts should be sent to the people who are currently entitled to receive money from the trust, in addition to being filed in court in the case of a court trust.

The trustee's responsibility includes keeping the trust funds well invested, paying taxes and expenses, and making payments to people as directed by the document that created the trust. Often those provisions may leave the trustee no choice as to whether or not to make payments. For example, the trustee may be directed to pay all of the income to you. In that situation, if the trustee refuses to pay you the income, you should ask a lawyer how to compel the trustee to comply with the terms of the document creating the trust. In other situations, the document may give the trustee power to determine whether or not payments should be made to you. For example, the trustee may be directed to pay principal to you when it is needed for your "reasonable support and maintenance." In that situation, if the trustee refuses to pay principal to you, this refusal may merely reflect his or her belief that the money is not needed for your support. However, you should consult a lawyer if you believe the trustee's position is wrong, given the facts of your case.

Other trust agreements and wills give the trustee the power to determine not only the amount to be paid out but also to whom it should go. For example, the trustee may be directed to pay both income and principal to one or more descendants of the person who created the trust. In this situation, the trustee can determine both which of the descendants to pay and how much each should receive. However, the language of the particular trust may place some limits on the trustee's ability to make these choices. If you believe the trustee is acting unfairly, you may wish to ask a lawyer about your rights in the matter.

If the trust is a court trust, you may be asked to approve the trustee's account before it is filed in court for approval. If it is not a court trust, you still may be asked to approve the trustee's account for a given period because the trustee does not wish to be compelled, at some distant future date, to defend his or her actions. In either case, before approving the account, you should be satisfied that the payments for which the trustee claims credit were proper and that the property of the trust was handled with reasonable care. When you approve an account, you are giving up your right to object to what the trustee did and to claim that the trustee is liable to the trust for damage it suffered from his or her acts (or failure to act).

Sometimes there may be no way for someone interested in a trust to know, from the information given in the trust account, that improper payments were made. This was true in one case in which income was payable to a widow until she remarried. She did remarry but managed to keep the trust company from finding this out. So it continued to pay her the trust income, and these payments were shown on the trust accounts without giving her new married name. The other beneficiary approved the accounts, but when the facts came to light this approval was held to be nonbinding because the trust company had made no effort to determine whether the widow had remarried. The trust company had to repay the money it had paid to the widow after her remarriage, with interest, amounting to over $300,000.

As with an estate, your approval of an account covers not merely the sale of trust property but also the failure to make sales when it would have made sense to do so. However, again as with an estate, the trustee is simply expected to act with reasonably good judgment, not to make no mistakes. If you believe the trustee has failed to use good judgment, you should promptly ask a lawyer what steps you should take to protect your interests.

Trusts may last for a short time or a long time, depending on the terms of the will or trust agreement. In almost all states, the maximum period allowed is until twenty-one years after the deaths of members of a group who were living when the trust was created. (Lawyers refer to this limit as the "Rule Against Perpetuities," because it prevents the creation of perpetual trusts except for charities.) For example, the person who created the trust may provide that it shall continue until twenty-one years after the deaths of all of his children who were living when the trust was created. Depending on the ages of his children at the time and on their life spans, the trust may last for a very long time indeed. It is not unknown for trusts to continue for eighty years or more.

In a trust that lasts a long time, if one of the original trustees is an individual rather than a bank or trust company, it is likely that he or she will have died or resigned because of ill health before the trust has ended. Thus, the will or trust agreement should either state who is to become successor trustee or provide a procedure for the remaining trustee (if there is one) or the beneficiaries to appoint one. If no successor is named, or the named successor declines to be trustee, the court can be asked to appoint a trustee.

Family trustees often serve without compensation, but professionals naturally expect to be paid for their services. There is such a wide variation between states as to how fees are computed that it is difficult to generalize. Annual fees may range from ½ percent to as much as 1 percent or more of the value of the principal. A fee based on the value of the trust property may be combined with a fee on the income of the trust. In addition, there often is a distribution fee, based on the value of any principal that is paid out while the trust continues or that is distributed when it ends. Banks and trust companies often publish fee schedules based either on a state law fixing fees or on the practice of others in the area. If the fee schedule is not provided by law, court approval of the fee requested by the trustee may be required, unless it is agreed to by the beneficiaries.

As in the case of estates, when you receive money or property from a trust, it may or may not be subject to income tax. This is because money or property you receive from a trust is not included in income for tax purposes unless it is considered to represent income earned by the trust. The trustee should tell you what part of the money or property you receive from a trust should be included in your income for tax purposes and what part is considered to be nontaxable principal. If you receive property, such as securities, rather than money, the trustee should also tell you the cost of the property for tax purposes so that you can figure your gain or loss when it is sold.

PART III

HOW YOU CAN
HELP YOUR FAMILY
(AND OTHERS)
WHILE YOU LIVE

$\mathbf{M}$ANY PEOPLE *do not want to make any big gifts while they live. Often this is because they do not believe they have more than enough money to meet their own needs. This part of the book is for people who feel that they can afford to help members of their family or other people during their own lifetime.*

If you can afford to do so, there may be several important reasons for helping family members and others now. There may be specific needs to be met— for support, education, or medical care—that cannot wait until later. Furthermore, if you provide financial help while you are living, you have a chance to see how it is used. In addition to the satisfaction of seeing what having more money can mean to someone you care about, you have the opportunity to experiment with different methods of providing help. This will give you a better idea of how you will want to leave your money. For example, you may want to help a grandson. You can do so in many ways—by giving him money, by paying his bills, or by giving money to one of his parents as custodian or guardian for him. If you experiment with these various methods while you are living, you can see how they work out.

Finally, disposing of part of your wealth while you live is an important way to save taxes, both income taxes during your life and estate and inheritance taxes after your death. You save income taxes by causing the income earned on property you give away to be taxed to someone in a lower income tax bracket. You save estate and inheritance taxes by reducing the amount of your wealth to be taxed. Because the importance of saving taxes depends very much on the amount of income and property you have to work with, taxes are discussed separately in parts 5 and 6. This part will deal with the different ways in which you can help others financially, whether or not you are concerned with tax problems.

The method that most people think of first is that of making a gift. There are various ways to make gifts of different kinds of property, and these are explored in chapter 7. Substantial gifts often are made through trusts, so that the trustee receives and holds the property for the benefit of whoever the person who set up the trust wants to help. Chapter 8 shows how to use trusts to make gifts. But there are also ways to help others without making a gift. These alternatives are the subject of chapter 9.

CHAPTER 7

Gifts

MANY PEOPLE are not fully aware of the legal formalities that are required to make a gift. Many small gifts are made simply by handing the item to the recipient. But the rules are more complicated for gifts of more valuable items, such as real estate or stock. If you do not follow them carefully, there is always the risk that someone may argue after your death that a gift you made during your life was legally ineffective. If that argument prevails, the property will be disposed of as part of your estate and may pass to someone other than the person you wanted to have it.

What does the law require in order to avoid this?

To make a gift, you must intend to do so and must deliver the property to the recipient (or someone acting for him or her). The recipient, in turn, must accept the gift. What these rules mean in any given case depends on the kind of property that is involved and whether or not the recipient is a minor or legally incompetent for other reasons.

There is also a special kind of gift, known as "gifts causa mortis," to which different rules apply. These gifts are made in anticipation of imminent death from some particular cause and can be revoked at any time prior to the donor's death. For example, someone about to undergo major surgery may deliver valuables to a friend or relative saying, "If I don't come back from the hospital, these are yours." Gifts causa mortis ordinarily should be used only in an emergency, when there is too little time to change your will, because it may be hard to prove that the gift was actually made. Such problems can be avoided by making the gift by your will instead.

Gifts may be made either directly or through a trust, and may be made to one person or to more than one. The advantages in making gifts through a trust are discussed in chapter 8.

Gifts of Different Kinds of Property

Different methods are used to give different kinds of property. It is important to use the right method in order to be sure that the gift will be legally effective.

The major forms of property that you may want to give away include:

Gifts

1. Real estate
2. Intangible personal property—chiefly corporate stock, bonds, notes, and life insurance
3. Tangible personal property—furniture, jewelry, automobiles, and similar items
4. Money (or a check)

Real Estate

To make a gift of real estate, you need a lawyer to prepare a document, called a deed. Homemade deeds often lead to lawsuits because there usually is no piece of paper that represents the title to real estate. For shares of stock or automobiles, on the other hand, there is a certificate showing who is the owner. Although you can buy a form deed at a legal stationery store, you need a lawyer to fill in the blanks correctly.

A deed does not represent ownership. Whether it transfers any interest in the property depends on whether the person who made the deed had any interest to transfer. Someone who buys real estate relies on an attorney or a title insurance company, depending upon local practice, to check the public records to see whether the seller actually owned the property described in the deed. Those records, in the office of the Recorder of Deeds or some similar local official, show what papers have been filed that affect the ownership of real estate.

You should deliver the deed to the person to whom you are giving the property. That person should then file it promptly with the Recorder of Deeds or whatever public official is responsible for placing deeds on record.

Intangible Personal Property

Intangible personal property refers to items that are valuable for what they represent, rather than in and of themselves. For example, a stock certificate is valuable not as a piece of paper but rather because it represents ownership of shares in a corporation. The kinds of intangible personal property that are most commonly given are corporate stock, bonds, notes, and life insurance.

Corporate Stock. Ownership of shares of corporate stock is represented by a stock certificate, which can be transferred by sending the certificate to the transfer agent of the corporation with a so-called stock power signed by the person whose name is on the certificate. The form that is printed on the back may be used for this purpose, with the name of the recipient filled in. Ordinarily, however, a separate document is used, so that if there is any error, the stock power can be destroyed and a new one substituted, without the error having been recorded on the back of the certificate itself. You can obtain stock powers from your broker.

Your signature on the stock power must be guaranteed to be genuine either by a commercial bank or trust company or by a brokerage firm that is a member of the New York Stock Exchange, just as if you were selling the shares. The stock power and stock certificate (if a separate document is used) can then be forwarded, each in a separate envelope, to the transfer agent, who will issue a new certificate in the name of the person to whom you are making the gift. Separate envelopes are a precaution to guard against the possibility that the stock power and stock certificate might get into the hands of someone who would seek to transfer your shares into another person's name.

If you do not have a stock certificate for shares you own, it may be because the shares are being held for you by a broker or other custodian. In that case, the custodian can tell you what is required to transfer the shares. In some cases, a letter from you may suffice; in others, a signed stock power may be required, just as if you had possession of the stock certificate yourself.

Bonds. Unlike shares of stock, bonds may either be "registered" or "bearer." In the case of a registered bond, a certificate which represents ownership of the bond can be transferred by signing a "bond power," similar to a stock power. A bearer bond is transferred by delivery of the bond itself, so that changes in ownership need not be recorded. It will have coupons attached to be turned in for the payment of interest as it comes due. Bond coupons are collected through a bank.

Notes. A note is a piece of paper containing a promise to pay money on a specified date. Ordinarily, the note is payable by its terms to a named individual or corporation. It can be transferred, like a check, if endorsed by the owner (called the payee).

Life Insurance Policies. To make a gift of a life insurance policy, you need to complete a form provided by the insurance company, which is then filed with the company. The policy can be handed over directly to the recipient.

Tangible Personal Property

Many people give various kinds of tangible personal property. Some common examples are furniture, automobiles, and jewelry. Usually such gifts are made without using any document. The donor merely hands the property to the recipient with intent to make a gift, and the recipient accepts it. Automobiles (and boats) are in a special class, however, because state law usually provides for a certificate of title to be issued by a state official when the car is first licensed. In order to transfer ownership, the certificate of title must be signed and notarized. After this has been done, the certificate is delivered to the appropriate state official, who will issue a new certificate to the donee.

Suppose you want to give property that you can't conveniently hand over. The property may, for example, be too bulky. Or it may be held by someone else, as in the case of a painting that has been loaned to a museum. In these situations, your lawyer should prepare a "Deed of Gift" (like a deed to real estate) for you to sign and deliver to the recipient.

Sometimes gifts have been made by what is called "symbolic" delivery. For example, the contents of a chest may be given by delivering the key, if both the donor and recipient live in the house where the chest is located. This method of delivery is sometimes used to make a gift of the contents of safe deposit boxes, but it should not be relied on for this purpose. Although a court may hold that delivery of the key to the box is evidence of intent to make a gift of its contents, such a gift may readily be challenged. A safer course is to remove the items from the box and hand them to the recipient. Of course, if any of the items is a certificate for securities or for ownership of an automobile, the usual procedure for transferring such property should be used.

Money

Gifts of currency present no problems but a gift of a check may, if the donor who wrote the check dies before it has been cashed. Until a check is cashed, such a gift remains incomplete.

Gifts to More Than One Person

Suppose your gift is to more than one person. You may want to give your house to your children. Or you may want to give your house to your daughter for her life and then to her children.

In the first situation, where you want the recipients to enjoy the property together at the same time, it may be entirely reasonable to make a gift to them in either of the two relevant ways described in chapter 4 for holding title to property, as joint tenants or tenants in common. Which way you choose will depend on what you want to have happen to your property when one child dies. If you want his interest to go to the other children, you should make the gift to the children as "joint tenants with right of survivorship and not as tenants in common," or whatever language your lawyer recommends to achieve this result under the law of your state. If you want the share of a child who dies to pass under his will or to go to his heirs if he leaves no will, you should make the gift to the children as "tenants in common."

In the second situation, where you want the property to go first to one recipient, your daughter, and then to the other recipients, her children, you usually should use a trust. If you don't use a trust, you will be creating what lawyers call a "legal life estate." This means, in the context of our example, that during your daughter's life she is entitled to occupy the property or to collect the rents and must pay the taxes, and that on her death the property passes to her children.

The problem with a legal life estate is that the day may come when your daughter no longer wants to live in your house, perhaps because she is moving to another part of the country or to a nursing home. Your daughter may want to sell the house at that point. But because her children all have an interest in the property, if they are adults she must obtain all of their signatures in order to sell. Depending on state law, it may also be necessary for the spouses of any married children to sign as well. Someone whose signature is needed may refuse. If the house were held in trust, only the trustee's signature would be required. The situation becomes even more complicated if some of the children are minors who can act only through a guardian. In that case, court action is likely to be required to complete the sale of the house.

What has just been said about real estate is even more true if your gift is stock, given to your daughter for life and then to her children. The legal rules governing arrangements of this kind are less settled than in the case of real estate and are more likely to lead to court proceedings. A trust would therefore be a much clearer arrangement here as well.

When to Make Gifts to a Trustee, Custodian, or Guardian

If you are making a gift to a minor, any large amount of property should be given to a guardian, custodian, or trustee, as a minor cannot make legally binding contracts. For example, if a minor owns real estate, any lease he makes and any deed he gives to the property is subject to being canceled by him when he comes of age, if he wants to. The same is true if he owns stock or other investments. Although minors may be specifically authorized by state law to own life insurance policies, if the insured dies while the policy owner is still a minor, the insurance company usually will insist that a guardian be appointed and the proceeds of the policy be paid to the guardian.

If you are making a gift to an adult, there may be important reasons to make the gift in trust, rather than directly, if a large amount of property is involved. Trusts are one of the most important tools of estate planning, both to save taxes and to allow the donor to control who the property is to benefit and at what time.

The following chapter deals with the ways in which trusts (and trust substitutes) can work for you during your life.

CHAPTER 8

How to Use Trusts to Make Gifts

IF you want to make a gift of any large amount of property or money during your life, you should think hard about the advantages of making the gift through a trust. As was discussed in chapter 2, a trust is an arrangement that allows one or more individuals or a bank or trust company (or a combination of the two) to hold property for your benefit or for someone you want to help financially. The trustees are under a legal duty to dispose of the trust property, and the income it produces, in the way you directed in the document that set up the trust.

Let's use as our example Louise, a widowed or divorced grandmother who wants to make gifts to her daughter Jennie's minor child, Angela. If the amount Louise wants to give Angela is more than she is expected to spend in the near future, Louise usually should make the gift to someone else to hold for Angela—a guardian, custodian, or trustee. This is because Angela lacks the legal ability (and often the practical knowledge and experience) to handle more than a small amount in a checking account. Of course, if Louise is willing for the money to be held in a checking or savings account and to trust Angela to handle it, she doesn't need anyone to act for her.

Many women in Louise's situation have simply made the gift to Jennie, relying on her to use the gift for Angela's benefit. Often this method works well. But there are risks involved. Parents have been known to take money that was given them for their children and use it for themselves instead. And even if Louise has complete confidence that this will not happen, there is always the risk that Jennie's or her husband's creditors will get the money.

Your lawyer can advise you whether the amount you are giving is big enough to justify the trouble and expense involved in setting up a trust to make your gift.

Lifetime gifts in trust often are made to save taxes. Those which save income taxes do so by causing income to be shifted for tax purposes, so that instead of being reported in the tax return of the person who created the trust, it is reported either as income of the people who receive money or property from the trust or as income of the trust itself. To serve this income-shifting function, a trust must satisfy the tax rules discussed in chapter 13.

Some trusts that save income taxes also save estate taxes. They do so by keeping the property from being counted for federal estate tax purposes, under the rules discussed in chapter 15, when the person who set up the trust dies.

If you make a gift that is effective to save income taxes or estate taxes or both, it almost always is treated as a gift for purposes of the federal gift tax. If, however, the gift fits the definition of a "present interest," and if you do not give the same person more than $10,000 in the same year, the gift does not count for gift tax purposes (or generally for estate tax, unless it is insurance on your life and you die within three years).*

Let's assume that Louise, in our example, has more than enough property for her own needs and is mainly concerned with providing for her children, Jennie and Mark, and for Jennie's children. Louise also wants to make a gift to a charity. If she uses trusts to make her gifts, she has four major alternatives, each of which is discussed in a separate section of this chapter:

1. Present interest trusts (or custodianships or guardianships)
2. Short-term (Clifford) trusts
3. Long-term trusts
4. Charitable split-interest trusts

She will also need to decide who is to be trustee, and what property to transfer to the trust. These issues are the subject of the final two sections of the chapter.

In choosing her trustee, Louise should keep in mind that if she or someone whom the tax law re-

---

*The gift tax rules are covered in chapter 14.

gards as a "related or subordinate party" is trustee, Louise herself may be treated as owner of the trust for income tax purposes. In this situation, if the trustee has the power to decide how much income or principal to pay out, or to whom payments shall be made, Louise may be taxed on the income from the trust property. It is also possible if Louise is trustee, or has the power to appoint a successor trustee, that the property will be included in her taxable estate when she dies.

The examples in this chapter of trusts in which the trustee has the power to decide who and how much to pay do *not* discuss whether any limits must be placed on those powers for tax reasons. Depending on who is the trustee, limits may be needed in order to keep Louise from being taxed on the trust income,* or to keep the property from being included in her taxable estate.†

Present Interest Trusts, Custodianships, and Guardianships

If what Louise wants to do is to accumulate funds that her grandchildren can later use for college or for a down payment on a house, gifts of "present interests" may be a highly useful estate-planning tool, because of the exemption from the gift tax and

---

*These tax rules are discussed in more detail in chapter 13, pp. 212–15.
†See chapter 15, pp. 230–33.

estate tax described earlier. Louise has five main alternatives if she wants to make a present interest gift for the benefit of her minor granddaughter Angela. She can make the gift to a:

1. Guardian for Angela
2. Custodian for Angela
3. Minor's present interest trust (must give Angela the right to the entire trust fund at 21)
4. "Crummey" trust (must give Angela, or her guardian, the right to withdraw principal the year Louise adds it to the trust)
5. Trust for Angela's life

Although the first two alternatives do not involve trusts, they are commonly used.

Guardianship

EXAMPLE: Louise transfers property to Jennie "as guardian for Angela Stevens," after Jennie has been appointed as guardian by the court.

The time-honored way to make gifts to a minor is to make a gift to her guardian. If Jennie received such a gift as guardian for Angela, Jennie would hold the property for Angela's benefit.

Guardianships have two disadvantages that often lead people like Louise to use a custodianship or trust instead. First of all, a guardian's powers end when the minor comes of age. When this occurs depends on state law but it usually is at eighteen. The guardian is then required to turn the property over to the child, even though at that age the child may not have the maturity and judgment to handle money.

The second disadvantage is that in many states guardianships mean red tape. The guardian is required to file accounts in court, listing every item received or paid out, and often must get the court's approval to use the property for the benefit of the child in a particular way, such as to pay the child's orthodontist.

Nevertheless, Louise would be well advised to make her gifts to a guardian for Angela if she wants to give property that is not covered by the state custodianship statute. Often the state law that authorizes gifts to custodians only covers gifts of securities, life insurance, and money. In that case, if Louise wants to give something else, such as an interest in a painting, she cannot use a custodianship.

Custodianship

EXAMPLE: Louise transfers property to Jennie "as custodian for Angela Stevens under the State X Uniform Gifts to Minors Act."

A custodianship usually involves a good deal less red tape than a guardianship does. There is no need to file accounts in court, and the custodian may spend money he or she holds for the benefit of a child without having to go to court for approval. However, a custodianship is not a good way to give large amounts because it is a form set by law and cannot be tailor-made to your own case the way a trust can be. Suppose the custodian dies, either before or after your death, and before the child comes of age. The law of your state provides for a successor custodian, but it may not be the one you would have chosen. Or suppose that the child dies before coming of age. Again the law directs how the custodian will dispose of the property held for the child, but it may not be in the way you would have preferred.

As with a guardianship, the custodian's powers end when the child reaches a specified age—either eighteen or twenty-one, depending on state law. In some states guardianships end at eighteen but custodianships continue until twenty-one. Many people in Louise's situation feel that at either of those ages a grandchild is too young to handle a large amount of money.

An important advantage of a custodianship (or guardianship) over a trust is that a trust requires a separate income tax return. Income from property held by a custodian (or guardian) is simply treated as income of the child for whom the property is held. The child has a larger exemption than a trust does, and is taxed at lower rates. Also, it is much easier to prepare the child's individual income tax return than it is to cope with the complexities of a trust income tax form.

Minor's Present Interest Trust

EXAMPLE: Louise transfers property worth $10,000 to a trustee for the benefit of her granddaughter Angela. The terms of the trust follow the tax rules so that the gift is a "present interest" and qualifies for the $10,000 annual gift tax exclusion. The trustee is authorized to use income and principal for Angela's benefit until she reaches twenty-one, adding any excess income to principal at the end of each year. The trust may provide that when Angela reaches twenty-one, the principal and accumulated income shall be paid to her.

If Louise does not want to require this payment to be made, she must instead give Angela the right to demand payment within some reasonable time after reaching twenty-one, for example, within ninety days. The trust provisions must also require the trustee to tell Angela that she has this right. If Angela doesn't demand payment within that time, the trustee may continue to hold the property for her benefit until she reaches whatever later age Louise specifies, or even until Angela dies.

Thus as soon as Angela turns twenty-one, the trust principal and income will be hers if she asks for it (or automatically, if the trust ends at that time). If the terms of the trust require her to demand payment and she fails to do so, she may be taxed on the trust income whether or not it is paid to her, because she could have gotten whatever was in the trust by demanding it.

Until Angela reaches twenty-one, however, the trust income will be taxed to the trust unless it is paid to Angela or used for her benefit. Whether this saves taxes depends on whether Angela or the trust is in a higher income tax bracket. Often the trust will be in the higher bracket, unless Angela has other income. If the trust is in a higher bracket, the tax will be less if the trustee pays income to Angela or uses it for her benefit, so that she and not the trust will be taxed.

If trust income is used to pay for things the state law says Angela's parents must give her as part of her support, that part of the income will be taxed to the parents instead of to Angela herself, just as if the money had been paid to them directly. So the trustee should be careful to pay only those bills which are not for things Angela's parents are under a legal duty to pay for. For example, the trust income cannot be used to buy her everyday clothes. Not only would this make her parents taxable on that part of the trust income, but it arguably is a payment the trustee cannot legally make under the terms of the trust. To satisfy the gift tax requirements, the trust must provide that income and principal may be used only for Angela's benefit. It certainly is no benefit to her to have the trust pay expenses that her parents are legally required to pay.

Whether or not this tax treatment of items that parents are under a legal duty to pay for applies to private school tuition depends on the state. In at least one state, Rhode Island, parents are never legally obligated to provide private school education if trust income can be used for this purpose. However, if the parents promise to pay the tuition when they fill out Angela's application to the school, the trust income used to pay tuition is paying a bill of theirs by carrying out their contract with the school. If Angela's parents want income from her trust to be used to pay her tuition, they should be careful to make no such promise to the school themselves and they should have bills for tuition sent to the trustee or to Angela.

Usually a parent's obligation to support children ends at eighteen, although in at least one state, New York, it continues until twenty-one. Thus in most states Angela's trust can be used for her college expenses after she reaches eighteen without making her parents taxable on the income, as long as their obligation under state law to support her has ended and they do not sign a contract with the college to pay her tuition or other expenses.

Which other items are outside a parent's support obligation again depends on state law. Common examples may include paying for the child's orthodontia and vacation travel. If Angela's parents are not legally obligated to provide orthodontia, it may be particularly useful from a tax standpoint to pay for it from her trust. Her parents' income may be so large that they get no deduction for medical expenses, which must exceed 5 percent of "adjusted gross income" to be deductible. If most of Angela's income is from the trust, it usually will be much easier for her to satisfy the 5 percent test.

Vacation travel is a more complicated case under state law than orthodontia. Parents have a legal duty to feed and house their children. Providing meals and lodging on a vacation trip is part of that continuing obligation. The plane ticket is another matter and may not be part of the support that state law requires, even though meals are included in the fare.

The minor's present interest trust may be more trouble than it is worth if only a small amount of property will be put in the trust. I was once trustee of such a trust that had only about $3,000 in it, and the trust income tax returns and accounts were more work than any taxes that the trust saved could make worth doing. However, if Louise plans to make a series of annual gifts of $10,000, beginning when Angela is only a few years old, the trust can soon amount to $100,000. With accumulated income and a rising stock market, it may even reach $250,000 before Angela turns twenty-one. If that is Louise's plan, she is likely to want the trust to continue after Angela reaches twenty-one. This raises some problems.

In order to avoid federal gift tax complications, the trust has to give Angela the right to demand the principal and accumulated income when she reaches twenty-one. If it failed to give her that right, the gift would not qualify for the $10,000 annual gift tax exclusion. However, if Angela is given the right to take principal and accumulated income at twenty-one, she may take the money when she does not have the judgment and maturity to handle it wisely.

If, on the other hand, Angela is given the right and doesn't exercise it, she may be treated as the owner of the trust and taxed on the trust income, whether or not the trustee pays it to her. This is an area where the tax rules have not been finally settled, but there are serious risks for Angela. Because she has the right to demand principal, she may be treated for income tax purposes as if she had taken the principal out and created a trust of her own. She may be subject to the strict income tax rules applied to those who set up trusts for themselves,* instead of the liberal rules that apply to beneficiaries of trusts created by others.† In short, when Angela reaches twenty-

---

*See chapter 13, pp. 212–15.
†See chapter 17.

one the minor's present interest trust may present problems.

"Crummey" Trust

EXAMPLE: Louise transfers property to a trustee for the benefit of her granddaughter Angela. Angela or her guardian has the right to demand any property that Louise gives to the trust, within a reasonable time after Louise makes the gift, such as ninety days, and the trustee must notify Angela or her guardian of this right.

The trustee may use income and principal for Angela's benefit until she reaches thirty-five or whatever age Louise may prefer, adding any excess income to principal at the end of each year. The trust provides that the trustee shall pay the principal and accumulated income to Angela when she reaches thirty-five. If Louise prefers, the trust may continue for Angela's life.

The Crummey trust is named for a taxpayer who got a "present interest exclusion" for the gift tax for gifts to such a trust. The reason is that Angela's right (or her guardian's) to demand property given to the trust constitutes a "present interest."

Of course, if Angela or her guardian made such a demand each time Louise transferred property to the trust, the trust would merely serve as a pipeline carrying property from Louise to Angela, and there would have been no reason to create it at all. Often, however, neither Angela nor her guardian will make any demands. If a demand is made, it is likely to be for only a part of the property put in the trust, such as the amount required to pay Angela's income taxes.

Basically, the Crummey trust is like a minor's present interest trust that provides for payment of principal and income to a child on demand at age twenty-one, except that in the Crummey trust the demand must be made shortly after the gift is made, when the child is less likely to exercise the right. However, the fact that Angela has the right to take what is put in the trust means that she may be taxed on all of the trust income right from the start, whether or not it is paid to her.

The biggest objection to the use of the Crummey trust is not, in my opinion, the fact that the child may be taxed on the trust income she never receives. The trustee can use some of the income to pay Angela's taxes, so she need be no worse off as a result. But some day Angela will learn that she had the right each year to take the property that was added to the trust that year and make it her own, and that her rights to the major part of the trust property lapsed when she was too young to make a free, timely, and informed choice. Children in Angela's situation may be angry for a long time when they find this out.

Trust for a Minor Grandchild for Life

EXAMPLE: Louise transfers property to a trustee to pay the income to Angela for her life, and on Angela's death to pay the trust fund to other members of Louise's family.

This trust creates two separate interests. One is for Angela, who has the right to income for her life. The other is for other members of Louise's family, who will get the principal when Angela dies. Since Angela has the right to income, starting as soon as the trust is set up, she has the kind of interest that is a "present interest" for purposes of the $10,000 annual gift tax exclusion. The interests of other members of Louise's family are not, and therefore will count for gift tax and estate tax purposes. However, this might not be important. Even if Angela is a teenager, her interest will take up most of the value of the gift, and the interests of the others will have only a low value. For example, if Angela is sixteen when the gift is made, under the tables of the Internal Revenue Service, her life interest is worth over 97 percent of the total value of the gift. This means that if Louise gives $10,000 to the trust, she will get a gift tax exclusion of over $9,700 for Angela's interest. Less than $300 of the gift will count for gift tax and estate tax purposes.

Since the income must be paid to Angela, it will be taxed to her, not to the trust. Any capital gains will be taxed to the trust itself, because they are added to the trust principal.

The problem with getting the present interest exclusion for the gift tax in this way is that Angela must be given the income each year. If she is in her middle or late teens, that may not be a serious objection, because she will be able to spend the money herself or put it in a bank account. However, if she is a young child, it will be impractical to pay the income to her, and it will have to be paid to a guardian or custodian for her until she is older—which makes it all more complicated.

Short-Term (Clifford) Trusts

If Louise is in a high income tax bracket, she may want to save income taxes without giving up any of her income-producing property for good. She may believe that when she retires, for example, she will need the income from all of her property to live on. Meanwhile, she would like to use some of the income she doesn't need either to help her children, Jennie and Mark, during the early years when they are just getting started and could use more money, or to build up a fund for her grandchildren.

The kind of trust that will allow Louise to do this is named for a famous federal tax case the taxpayer lost. He set up a trust, with himself as trustee, and directed the trustee to return the trust property to him after five years. The Supreme Court held that because the time was so short, and because he had so much control as trustee, the trust income would be taxed to him even though he had no right to receive it.

Congress has since drawn the line at ten years and one day or the life of the beneficiary, whichever ends first. If the trust will last at least that long, the trust income won't be taxed to the person who set the trust up because of his or her right to get the principal back when the trust ends. The person may, however, be taxed because of the control that he or she (or someone else) has over the trust.

EXAMPLE: Louise transfers property to Mark as trustee to pay the income to Jennie for ten years and one day or until Jennie dies, then to return the principal (including capital gains) to Louise. Since the trustee has no choice as to who gets the income, Jennie, or even Louise herself, could be trustee without making Louise, rather than Jennie, taxable on the trust income.

Since Jennie has the right to the income, starting as soon as the trust is set up, Louise can get a present interest exclusion for the value of Jennie's interest in the trust, up to $10,000 each year Louise puts money in the trust.

This exclusion will cover a transfer by Louise of more than $10,000 in one year because her gift is only the value of Jennie's right to income from the trust for ten years, or until Jennie dies, whichever happens first. As this book goes to press, the tables that the Internal Revenue Service uses to value that right are based on an assumed 10 percent return, and give a value for Jennie's interest of about 61 percent of the amount transferred by Louise. (The tables used before December 1983 assumed a 6 percent return and should be checked for any later revisions before setting up a trust of this type).

In order to make maximum use of the annual exclusion, Louise may want to set up the trust one year and add to it over several more years, so that more than one year's exclusion will apply. If she wants to do this, the trust should be set up to last for more than ten years, so that there will still be ten years and one day to go when the last gift to the trust is made. Otherwise, the income from any property that Louise will get back sooner than that will be taxed to Louise.

Some lawyers would urge Louise either not to set up the trust or to make it a long-term trust, with no possibility of getting the principal back. They believe that it is impractical to make gifts to a Clifford trust that do not exceed the $10,000 present interest exclusion each year and still have enough in trust to make it worthwhile. Whether a Clifford trust makes sense for someone in Louise's situation is something for her to work out with her lawyer.

Long-Term Trusts

If what Louise wants is to provide for Jennie for her life and then have the property go to Jennie's children, a long-term trust may offer important advantages. Louise's basic alternatives are:

1. A trust that sets forth exactly who gets income and principal and how much. This is called a "nondiscretionary trust."
2. A trust that provides that one of the beneficiaries can determine who gets income and principal and how much. This is a "trust with powers of appointment," or "trust with beneficiary powers."
3. A trust that provides that the trustee can determine who gets income and principal and how much. This is called a "discretionary trust."

Each kind of long-term trust has important advantages over Louise's other option, which is to give the property to Jennie directly and hope that in due course it will go to her children. If that is what Louise wants, a trust is a far more reliable way to insure that it will happen.

If Louise gives property directly to Jennie, without using a trust, Louise loses control over it. Part or all of the property may never reach the grandchildren. Jennie may spend it, or it may pass to others.

In many states, for example, if Jennie is divorced the judge can transfer any of her property to her ex-husband. Today the risk is much greater that property Mark received from Louise would be assigned to his ex-wife than that property Jennie got would be assigned to her ex-husband. Although the Supreme Court has ruled that state laws dealing with assignment of property and payment of alimony on divorce must be "gender neutral," in practice an ex-wife is more likely to be able to establish a need for her ex-husband's property or for alimony than an ex-husband is. By the time Jennie gets a divorce, however, this may no longer be true, as women assume greater responsibility for the support of their families. So it is always possible that a court may decide that Jennie's ex-husband should be given part of Jennie's property to live on, even though it came from Louise.

If Jennie and her husband live in a community property state while married, the income from property Louise gives Jennie may all be community property. Even the principal may be treated as community property, for purposes of division on divorce or when Jennie dies, if she does not keep it segregated so that it can be proved to be her separate property.

In most non-community-property states, if Jennie's husband survives her, he is legally entitled to take a share of her estate, without regard to what may be provided in her will. This includes the part of her estate that came from Louise.

A long-term trust could minimize the risk that Louise's property would end up with Jennie's husband, her creditors, or the tax collector when she dies, without preventing Jennie from enjoying the property while she lives.

The trust may continue for as long as Louise wants, up to twenty-one years after the death of a reasonable number of people (named or described in the trust document) who are living when it is set up. Your lawyer can explain the rule limiting the length of time that a trust can continue, which lawyers refer to as the "Rule Against Perpetuities," and how it applies to your trust.

Nondiscretionary Trust

EXAMPLE: Louise may transfer property to a trustee to pay the income to Jennie for life. When Jennie dies, the income is payable to her children in equal shares (or to someone else for their benefit) until they reach twenty-one, when each of them gets a share of principal.

One advantage for Louise of a nondiscretionary trust like this one is that anyone can be the trustee without making the trust income taxable to her,* or having the trust property count as part of her taxable estate when she dies.† This even includes Louise herself, although the more cautious course is for her

---

*For a discussion of the relevant income tax rules, see chapter 13, pp. 212–15.

†The relevant estate tax rules are covered in chapter 15, pp. 230–33.

not to be trustee of her own trust because of the risk that the terms of the trust may give her some power that will make the trust income be taxed to her or cause the trust to be counted for federal estate tax purposes.

The big disadvantage of a nondiscretionary trust is that Louise cannot anticipate, in a trust that may last for fifty years or more, what the different needs of members of her family will be over the years. Jennie may need the income from the trust when Louise sets it up, but in time she may advance in a business or profession so that her income is quite large. In that situation, the income from the trust may not mean much to her, because she has to pay taxes on it in her high income tax bracket, and she may not spend what she has left after the tax is paid. From a tax standpoint, the effect is the same if her husband's income increases and, like most couples, they file a joint return. In either case, Jennie may wish that the trustee had the power to divert income from her to her children. Or if her children are too young to use it, she may prefer that the trustee could accumulate the income and pay it to them at a later time, perhaps when they are going to college or graduate school or buying a house.

The needs of each of Jennie's children also may differ. One child, as a result of illness or accident, may be very short of funds while the others are prospering and have no great need for money from Louise's trust.

Giving either the trustee or someone else the power to decide how much to pay, and to whom, with proper safeguards to avoid tax traps, allows the trust to be flexible and to be used the way Louise would have wanted over the years. No rigid division between income and principal or shares fixed in advance for different family members can take into account what the twists of fate may do to them over time. It has been said that the foresight of a genius is not equal to the judgment of an average person who is on the scene at the time. For this reason, I believe that all long-term trusts should have some powers built into them to provide flexibility in the light of changing circumstances.

Of course, those powers may have to be limited in some cases because of a tax objective that the trust is intended to serve. For example, if, when she sets the trust up, Louise wants to get a present interest exclusion for gift tax purposes for the value of Jennie's right to income, she cannot make the payment of income to Jennie depend on the exercise of a power by the trustee. But even in this case, it is possible to build in some flexibility by giving Jennie the power to make gifts of the trust property during her life. She also can be given the power in her will to change the provisions that are effective after her death, to allow her to change the terms of the trust to take into account changes in the needs of the children between the time Louise sets up the trust and the time Jennie revises her will.

Trust with Beneficiary Powers (or Powers of Appointment)

EXAMPLE: Louise may transfer property to a trustee to pay the income to Jennie for life. Jennie also is given the following powers over the trust property:

1. She may withdraw as much principal as is needed for her reasonable support and maintenance.
2. She may withdraw in addition not more than the greater of $5,000 or 5 percent of the value of the principal each year.
3. She may revise the provisions for her children and other descendants by her will.

This battery of powers over the trust property would not give Jennie as much control as she would have if she got the property directly, without a trust. She could not, for example, use all of it in one year to buy a diamond necklace or take a trip around the world. But if Jennie would not want to spend large amounts of principal anyway, the trust will allow her to do quite a lot with the money. Yet because she is not the owner of it, it may be impossible for her husband to claim a share if they are divorced or she dies; her creditors cannot reach more than she is entitled to receive under the terms of the trust; and when she dies, the taxes may be far less than if she had gotten the property outright and left it to her children. There may even be no tax to pay at all.

Of course, Louise does not have to give Jennie the complete package of powers in the example. The package merely shows that Jennie can be given a lot of control over the trust property without having any of it be subject to estate tax when she dies, except for the part she could have taken out at that time under her power to withdraw $5,000 or 5 percent of the value of the trust. Although the trust may be subject to the generation-skipping transfer tax when Jennie dies, there is a $250,000 exemption if the property passes to her children in the form required by the tax law.*

From Jennie's standpoint, the disadvantage of having this kind of a trust is that she is stuck with paying tax on all the income from the trust property for her life. She may need the income when the trust is set up, but the time may come when her income from other sources is so large that she would prefer to have the trust income either paid to her children or accumulated for their benefit. The trustee may be able to help in this situation by investing in securities or other assets which are likely to grow in value but which produce little current income. But this may not be a practical alternative if the trust consists of property that is not readily salable, or that cannot be sold without incurring a substantial capital gains tax.

If Jennie is concerned about the possibility that the trust may cause her to be taxed on more income than she needs, she may prefer to have Louise make the income payable to her only in the discretion of someone else as trustee, and to give the trustee the power to pay income to the children or to accumulate it in the trust if that seems advisable. Of course, Jennie cannot have the power to decide for herself whether income is to be paid to her or to the children or is to be accumulated, or she will be taxed on the full amount no matter where it goes. But the power to make this decision can be given to someone else who can be expected to keep Jennie's interests in mind.

---

*For an explanation of this tax, see chapter 16, pp. 249–52.

Discretionary Trust

EXAMPLE: Louise could transfer property to a trustee to pay income and principal at his discretion to Jennie and her descendants, or to apply it for their benefit.

Giving the discretionary powers over income to the trustee has the advantage for Jennie of keeping her from paying taxes on income she doesn't need or want. It also may be useful if Louise would prefer someone other than Jennie to decide whether income or principal should be paid to her.

The accumulated income may be subject to an additional tax when it is paid out, but generally not if it is paid to a descendant who was under twenty-one (or unborn) when the income was accumulated.*

Charitable Split-Interest Trusts

If Louise wants to make a gift to charity, there may be important tax advantages in combining the charity's gift with provisions for Louise herself or for her siblings or descendants. If she wants to do this, she has two major alternatives:

1. A charitable remainder trust, in which she or members of her family (or both) receive payments for their lives or for a period of years. After that time, the charity gets the principal and any accumulated income. (A pooled income fund may allow more than

---

* See the discussion of the throwback tax in chapter 17, p. 259.

one donor to contribute to a charitable remainder trust.)
2. A charitable lead trust, in which the charity's interest comes first and is followed by provisions for members of Louise's family.

Each trust offers important tax advantages over Louise's other alternative, which is to give the property to the charity directly, without a trust. Although a direct gift would not be subject to gift tax and would qualify for the income tax charitable deduction, Louise would lose the potential tax savings that a charitable split-interest trust could provide.

Charitable Remainder Trust

EXAMPLE: Louise may transfer property to a trustee to pay her each year for life either a fixed amount of money or a percentage of the current value of the principal. On her death, the principal, and any accumulated income, is payable to a charity.

If the amount paid to Louise each year is fixed, it is called an "annuity" and must be at least 5 percent of the value of the principal when the trust is created. If the amount paid to Louise is based on the current value of the principal, it is called a "unitrust amount" and must be at least 5 percent of the value of the principal or the trust income, whichever is less. The value is recomputed each year to determine the amount to be paid to her for that year.

If the annuity or unitrust amount is payable only to Louise herself, there is no gift tax when she sets the trust up, because you cannot make a gift to yourself. Her only gift is to a charity, and a charitable deduction is allowed for gift tax purposes. Louise is taxed on the income she receives from the trust. But she saves income taxes because she gets an income tax deduction for her gift to charity when she sets the trust up. Her deduction is for the amount of the estimated value of the charity's interest, under the tables used by the Internal Revenue Service.

The trust itself is generally exempt from income taxes. Thus, if Louise gives stock to the trust that goes up in value, the trustee can sell the stock and pay no income tax on the gain, even though the money received from the sale will be used as long as Louise lives to produce income to make payments to her. And if the trust's income is more than those payments, it pays no tax on the excess income, because any accumulated income on hand when Louise dies will go to charity.

Louise will pay income tax on the payments she receives from the trust, if those payments are either from income or from capital gains of the trust. But the trust will not increase her estate tax when she dies, because it is going to charity.

Louise could, if she wished, have the trust provide payments to a child or grandchild, either during Louise's life or after she had died. In that case, the value of the interest given to the child or grandchild would count for gift tax purposes. But in other respects, the trust would have the same tax advantages that would result if the payment went only to Louise herself.

149

Charitable Lead Trust

EXAMPLE: Louise may transfer property to a trustee to pay either a fixed amount of money each year (an annuity) or a percentage of the current value of the principal each year (a unitrust amount) to a charity for a period of years. At the end of that time, the trust may continue for the benefit of her family or the trust property may be turned over to them.

Only women who are wealthy themselves and whose children are well-off are likely to set up a charitable lead trust, because it means postponing any benefit to their families until after a period of time when the trust only benefits the charity. Few women are likely to want to do this, even though impressive savings in gift and estate taxes may be achieved as a result.

Generally, the only income tax advantage to a woman like Louise from setting up a charitable lead trust is that the income from the property she transfers to the trust will no longer be taxable to her. Ordinarily she does not get an income tax deduction for the value of the interest in the trust that is given to charity.

The important advantage that may be achieved is saving gift taxes. Louise will get a gift tax charitable deduction when she sets up the trust for the estimated value of the charity's interest, based on the tables of the Internal Revenue Service. As this book goes to press, those tables that the Internal Revenue Service uses to value the charity's interest are based on an assumed 10 percent return on the trust investments. (The tables used before December 1983 assumed a 6 percent return and should be checked for any later revisions before setting up a trust of this type.) In fact the trust may earn more than 10 percent. If that happens, the trust pays income tax on the excess over the amount distributed to the charity. What it accumulates over and above these required payments and taxes will eventually go to Louise's family.

Under the 10 percent tables now used by the Internal Revenue Service, if, for example, Louise transferred $250,000 to a trustee to pay a 10 percent annuity to a charity, or $25,000 a year, for thirty years, then to continue the trust for her family, the charity's interest would be valued at $235,673, leaving only $14,237 subject to gift tax after subtracting the charitable deduction for the gift. When the charity's interest ended, after the thirty years had gone by, there might be more than $250,000 for Louise's family if the trust had earned more than the 10 percent required to pay the annuity.

This would mean that Louise had provided a large sum for her family, at a low gift tax cost. Of course that gift tax is payable when the trust is set up, and her family will not benefit for thirty years. If you are interested in setting up such an arrangement, you should get your lawyer's advice as to whether it makes sense in your case.

Who Should Be Trustee

In choosing trustees, Louise must comply with three sets of tax rules:

1. One set treats her as owner of a trust for income tax purposes if either she or a "related or subordinate party" has certain powers to make payments from the trust.*
2. Another set requires trust property to be counted in figuring her estate tax if she, as trustee, (or a successor trustee she can appoint) has certain powers over the trust.†
3. A third set creates tax problems for the trustee if he or she has the power to pay income or principal to himself or herself or to support his or her dependents.‡

Louise generally can satisfy all of these tax rules in one of two ways. She can limit the trustee's powers and have whoever she wants as trustee. Or she can give the powers she wants to a trustee who is not related or subordinate and hence will not be caught by any of the rules alluded to here.

Factors other than tax problems should enter into Louise's choice of trustees. These factors are discussed in chapter 19.

What Property Should Be Transferred to the Trust

In deciding what property to transfer to the trust, Louise should take a number of factors into account. To a large extent, her decision will depend on what she is trying to use the trust to accomplish.

* See chapter 13, pp. 212–15.
† See chapter 15, pp. 232–33.
‡ See chapter 16, pp. 245–46.

If she is setting up a short-term (Clifford) trust to save income taxes by causing trust income to be taxable either to the people who get money from the trust or to the trust itself, she can get a bigger tax advantage if she uses property that produces a high income. This is because for gift tax purposes, the value of her gift is not based on the actual income from the property but rather on an imaginary 10 percent return under the present Internal Revenue Service tables. If she gives property that is yielding 12 percent, she will get more income off her tax return than if she gave property of the same value that was yielding only 10 percent.

If she wants to get the property of a long-term trust out of her estate so that it will not be counted for estate tax purposes when she dies, she may want to choose property that is likely to go up in value over the years, so that more will be out of her estate when the time comes to determine the estate tax.

The choice of property also is affected by whether or not she expects it to be sold during her life, and what her basis (cost used to figure gain or loss on a sale) in the property is for income tax purposes.*

---

*For a discussion of basis, see chapter 13, pp. 210–11.

CHAPTER 9

How to Help People without Making Gifts

LET'S TAKE Louise again, a divorced or widowed grandmother with children and grandchildren whom she would like to help financially. If she does so by making gifts, she may end up paying gift tax. And if she uses a gift in trust to make part of her income taxable to one of her children instead of to her, the trust has to last for at least ten years or for the life of the child (whichever is shorter) before she can get the trust property back.

None of these tax problems will come up if she can help her family in other ways without making a gift. For example, she may be able to send business to one of her children or pass on opportunities to make favorable deals. She also may be able to help handle a child's business or investments without charging a fee. And Louise may have property that she can let her child use, either rent-free or at a bargain rental. In general, none of these arrangements have been held by the courts to amount to making a gift, for tax purposes.

There are two other important ways to help others, which require more formal planning, namely, loans and sales for annuities.

Loans

EXAMPLE: Louise lends $100,000 to her daughter Jennie, who invests the money or uses it to make a down payment on a house. Jennie signs a note in which she promises to pay Louise $100,000 on demand. No interest is due unless Jennie fails to pay the note when Louise requests it.

In recent years, loans such as this have been one of the most popular ways for people like Louise to help their children. It is clear that the $100,000 is not a gift unless Louise does not expect the loan to be repaid. So this is a way to give a child money he or she needs without making a gift of the money.

What is uncertain is whether the value of the use of the $100,000, during the time Jennie has the money, is a gift by Louise to Jennie. If Jennie had borrowed $100,000 from a bank, she would have paid a lot of interest. If she borrows from Louise instead and pays no interest, or less than a bank would charge, has Louise made a gift to Jennie of all or part of the interest?

A federal court of appeals decided in 1978 that an interest-free loan like this is not a gift of the interest that could have been charged on the money loaned, even though the loans in that case amounted to $18 million. However, in 1982 a different federal court of appeals held that such loans are indeed gifts by the lender of the value of the use of the money loaned.

To settle the conflict between these two court decisions, the Supreme Court heard arguments in the later case November 1, 1983. The Court is expected to decide sometime in 1984 which court of appeals is correct. In the meantime, Louise should assume that her loan may be treated as a gift to Jennie of the interest on the money loaned, for purposes of the gift tax.

But even if the Supreme Court decides that the 1982 decision is right, an interest-free loan may still be an attractive way for Louise to help Jennie. In our example, if the interest rate the Internal Revenue Service uses to determine the amount Louise has given is 10 percent or less and Louise makes no other gifts to Jennie, her gift each year the loan is outstanding will be covered by the $10,000 exclusion for gift tax purposes.

At the same time, the loan may save income taxes. If Louise had loaned the money to someone else and collected interest, she would have paid income tax on the interest in her own high income tax bracket. If Jennie makes the loan instead, with money supplied by Louise, Jennie may be in a much lower income tax bracket so that she pays less tax on the interest she collects than Louise would have paid if the interest had come to her instead.

Of course, Louise also could have caused part of her income to be taxed to Jennie by making a gift of income-producing property to a short-term (Clifford) trust for Jennie. But that would have required Louise to get a lawyer to draft the trust agreement, and she could not get the property back for at least ten years or until Jennie's death, whichever came first. Using an interest-free loan instead means that Louise does not have to commit herself for any specific length of time, in order to shift income for tax purposes. Whenever she wants the money back, all she has to do is ask Jennie for it.

Admittedly, there is always the risk that Jennie will be unwilling or unable to repay the loan. If Louise is concerned about this possibility, she should get some security from Jennie when she makes the loan, such as a mortgage or trust deed on Jennie's house.

What interest rate will the Internal Revenue Service use in figuring the amount of Louise's gift, if the Supreme Court decides that when you make an interest-free loan you make a gift of the interest? It may use the so-called prime rate, charged by banks to their best borrowers. This would be an additional break for Louise, because Jennie could not borrow from a bank at that low an interest rate. The prime rate changes rather frequently, so to be on the safe side, Louise should assume that the rate may be somewhat higher than what the banks are charging when she makes the loan.

Interest-free loans should not be made by someone like Louise to a trust that she has set up to get income from property off her income tax return. Her ability to demand payment of the loan gives her too much power over the trust property, and she may be taxed on the trust income just as if she owned the trust.

You should ask your lawyer how long you can wait to collect any loan you make before collection will be barred under state law. For example, the time in which you can sue to collect a note that is payable on demand may be limited to five years from the date you make the loan. Before the five years have gone by, you should get a new note, or take whatever other steps your lawyer recommends, to keep collection from being barred. Otherwise, when the five years expire, you will have made a gift of the amount you loaned, and may have to pay a gift tax.

Sales for Annuities

The kind of sale that may be most useful to Louise in helping her children without making a gift is a sale for an annuity, a regular payment by the buyer every year, or more often, for the life of the seller. Not everyone in Louise's situation should make this kind of sale. It should be gone into only after careful consideration of the consequences by you and your lawyer.

EXAMPLE: Louise owns vacant land, which is valuable for development as a residential subdivision. The land cost her $100,000, but today is worth $500,000. Louise sells the land to Jennie in return for Jennie's promise in writing to pay her an annuity of $70,700 per year for life. If Louise is 63 years old when the sale is made, under the actuarial tables the Internal Revenue Service is using as this book goes to press, the annuity that Jennie has agreed to pay to Louise is approximately equal in value to the land being sold. So Louise is not making a gift when she sells the land to Jennie on these terms. But the tax consequences may be very favorable, particularly if Louise is in failing health and does not live long after making the sale.

When Louise receives the first $70,700 payment from Jennie, she will treat part as tax-free recovery of her cost for the land, and the balance as taxable income. Part of this income will be capital gain until she has reported a total of $400,000 as gain on her income tax returns. What that part is, and how long it will take Louise to report the $400,000 as gain, is unclear. As this book goes to press, the Internal Revenue Service has not finished updating its actuarial tables for annuities, but is expected to do so in 1984.

If Louise lives longer than the time required to report the $400,000 as gain, the part of any later payments that is not tax-free is ordinary income, instead of being capital gain. The important point, though, is that property with a value of $500,000 has been gotten out of her estate without making a taxable gift. What she receives from Jennie each year will be included in Louise's estate when she dies, if she doesn't spend or give away the money before then. But if she lives only a short time, there won't have

159

been many $70,700 annuity payments from Jennie to be taxed in Louise's estate.

Sales for annuities may produce such favorable results because the annuity is valued without paying any attention to Louise's actual health and life expectancy unless she is practically at death's door, and because the interest rate the Internal Revenue Service uses, as this book goes to press, is 10 percent. This means that the annuity may in fact be worth a great deal less than the land but still will be treated as equal in value for federal gift tax purposes.

The Internal Revenue Service may change the interest rate used to value annuities. You should check with your lawyer to see what rate would apply before making a sale for an annuity.

From Louise's standpoint, the most important disadvantage in selling her land to Jennie for an annuity is that the tax rules make it unwise for Jennie to give Louise a mortgage or trust deed on the land to secure the payments due her. This means that Jennie could sell the land and spend the money, or that Jennie's other creditors could have the land sold to pay her debts. So Louise should not make the deal unless she has enough confidence in Jennie to assume these risks. There also will be complications if Jennie dies before Louise, because part of Jennie's estate will have to be set aside to pay Louise's annuity.

From Jennie's standpoint, one disadvantage to the deal is that she cannot get any income tax deduction for interest, although part of the payments she makes to Louise represents interest. There is also the risk that Louise will live longer than anyone expects, so that Jennie may have to make more annuity payments than she anticipated.

There are additional complications if the land has a building or other improvements on it, which should be explored by Louise and Jennie with their lawyers before they make the deal.

PART IV

HOW TO DISPOSE
OF YOUR PROPERTY
UPON YOUR DEATH

You ARE NEVER *without a plan to dispose of your property when you die. The state intestacy laws provide a plan for everyone who does not make one of his or her own. But do these laws give you the plan you want? Usually the answer is no, because the state's plan cannot take into account the particular facts of your case. Only a tailor-made plan can do that for you.*

If you choose to have such a plan of your own, the most important document you use may be either a will or a revocable trust agreement. Wills are by far the most common estate-planning tool. And even if you rely on a revocable trust agreement as a major part of your personal financial plan, you still need a will. Therefore, chapter 10 deals with why you need a will and what it can—and cannot—do for you.

In recent years, revocable trusts are increasingly being used as the most important document. This is because the revocable trust may be a convenient way to handle your money while you live and also save both time and money in disposing of your property after you die. These and other possible advantages of revocable trusts (as well as possible disadvantages) are covered in chapter 11. Finally, chapter 12 deals with the ways either a trust under your will or a revocable trust may be used to dispose of your property after your death.

CHAPTER 10

What a Will Can—and Cannot— Do for You

WHAT HAPPENS if you die without a will? In legal terms you die "intestate." The plan provided by the intestacy law of the state you live in will then control disposing of your property and choosing the person who will handle your estate.

If you die without a will when you live in one state and own land in another, the land will be disposed of under the law of the state where it is located. Your securities and other property will be disposed of under the law of the state where you live.

To avoid this situation you must have a will. This chapter explains a number of things you need to know about wills:

1. How state law disposes of your property if you die without a will

165

2. What a will can do for you
3. What it takes to make a valid will
4. What a will cannot do for you
5. What may be included in a will
6. How to change your will

What It Means to Die Intestate

The state legislature may have read your mind and provided the exact plan that you want to dispose of your property. In that case, you still need to make a will in order to choose the person who will act as executor in handling your estate and carrying out your plan and to give that person the broader powers that will help in doing the job.

But it is very likely that the state legislature did not read your mind about what to do with your property. To begin with, the relevant law probably was passed long before you were born. Although it may have been revised in recent years, the revisions cannot reflect each person's individual preferences. So you should see a lawyer to make your own will. Don't rely on the legislature to do the job for you. To a lesser extent, this also applies to the form will provided by law in at least one state, California, although it does leave blanks for you to fill in. It may be useful for people who are unwilling or unable to pay a lawyer to prepare a will.

I emphasize: have a lawyer do the job. Homemade wills are likely to end up in court; wills involve

too many legal rules for someone without legal training to handle them.

EXAMPLE 1: Sally, aged forty, is killed in an auto accident, leaving her husband, Tom, and three minor children. She had no will because she didn't
expect to die so young. She and Tom own a
house as "joint tenants" and have a joint checking account. Her only other property is stock, in
her name alone, worth $60,000, and her share of
the furniture.

Because Tom survived her, the house and the
joint checking account are now his alone. Tom
will become the court-appointed administrator
to handle Sally's estate and may have to file a
surety bond, at the estate's expense, to guarantee his faithful performance of his duties. The
stock—after payment of any debts Sally owes,
any estate and inheritance taxes that may be
due, and the expenses of administering the estate—will be divided among Tom and the children. Under a typical state law, Tom will get
one-third and the children will each get two-
ninths. The state law may give Sally's half interest in the furniture to Tom, but if not, it also may
be divided among him and the children.

For Sally, the state's plan gives her property to the
people she is most interested in helping, but it does
so in a way that will make handling her property
unnecessarily complicated and expensive. Tom will
have to become court-appointed guardian for the
children and will be able to use their shares of her
estate for their benefit only after getting the court's

approval. Tom is a logical candidate to be guardian, but in at least one state he is disqualified because his financial interest in the estate is opposed to that of the children.

Many women in Sally's situation would prefer to leave their property to Tom outright and rely on him to take care of the children. They would also name Tom as executor and authorize him to administer the estate without filing a surety bond, thereby saving an expense for the estate, if a surety bond would otherwise be required by law.

Of course, this does not provide for the chance that Sally and Tom may die together in the same accident. In that case, Sally would not only have her securities to dispose of but also her half interest in the family home and checking accounts. If there is no proof as to which joint owner was the survivor, state law usually will dispose of half of the property as if it belonged to each of the joint owners. In that situation, Sally probably would have wanted to set up a trust to handle the shares of the children until they are old enough to manage their own property.

Sally would also name guardians for her children. If Tom survives her, no guardian will be needed while he is living. But Sally should name guardians to provide for the chance that he may die first or shortly after she dies, instead of leaving the choice of guardian to be made by a court.

EXAMPLE 2: Louise, aged sixty-two, dies of a heart attack. She had no will because she wanted to avoid paying a lawyer to draw one up for her. She was a widow with two children: Jennie, who has four children of her own; and Mark, who is divorced and childless. Mark makes a lot of money and never spends his income. Jennie and her husband have been hard-pressed trying to raise four children on one paycheck.

Louise's estate consists of her house, furniture, and securities worth a total of $200,000. Everything will be divided equally between Mark, who doesn't need the money and has no room in his apartment for more furniture, and Jennie, who needs both.

For Louise, the state's plan does not give her property to the people she is most interested in helping now: Jennie and Jennie's children. If Louise had made a will, she could have taken the different needs of her children into account without cutting Mark out altogether. For example, she could have set up a trust that would give Jennie and her children the income until the children had all been educated. After that there could be equal shares for Jennie and Mark. Louise could also have given Mark any furniture he particularly wanted, with the balance to go to Jennie.

As these examples show, the first reason for making a will usually is to change the shares provided in the state's plan for people who die intestate. You are not completely free to make your own plan if your husband survives you, because state law usually provides a minimum share that cannot be taken away from him if he objects. If he does not want to accept the provisions of your will, he can claim his minimum share of your estate under state law, often one-third if you leave descendants or one-half if you don't.* In the eight community property states—Arizona, California, Idaho, Louisiana, Nevada, New Mexico, Texas, and Washington—the minimum share for a surviving spouse is the one-half of the community property that he or she owned while both spouses were living, but usually does not include any part of the separate property of the spouse who died.

Generally, you need not make any provision for your children, as long as your will shows that you intended to leave them out. As was discussed in connection with Example 1, a woman may choose to disinherit her children and leave everything to her husband, if he survives her, in order to simplify the handling of her estate.

Many people believe it is necessary to leave a child $1. Payment of such a legacy will create additional paperwork. It is better merely to state "I intentionally make no provision for my son George." Often a reason, such as "having previously provided for him in other ways," may be added. But it is unwise to give a reason that is critical of George, because there have been successful suits for libel by will.

What a Will Can Do for You

The most important thing a will can do for you is to direct who gets your property, and at what time. It should also name the executor who will handle your

---

*See p. 66, for a discussion of husband's rights.

estate and carry out your plan. If you have (or may have when you die) any minor children, your will should name guardians for them. And if you have the power to dispose of property you don't own (what lawyers call a "power of appointment") which can be exercised by will, your will should either exercise the power or say that you do not intend to do so. In that case, the property will pass under the provisions of the document that gave you the power.

Direct Who Gets Your Property

Your will can merely divide up your estate in shares, the way the state law would have if you made no will. Or you can leave all of your property to one person if you wish. But many women prefer to deal with their property in more detail than that. Ways to use trusts for this purpose are illustrated in chapter 12.

Name Your Executor

Your will should name the executor who will handle the administration of your estate. That is the procedure by which debts, taxes, and administration expenses are paid and whatever is left is transferred to the people you name in your will. Depending on the law of your state, it may also be desirable to give your executor additional powers to carry out the job, beyond those given by state law.

You do not have as much freedom in choosing an executor as you do in choosing who will receive shares in your estate. Some states will not allow a nonresident individual to serve as executor and others will do so only if a resident is appointed coexecutor. Banks and trust companies incorporated in other states also may not be allowed to act as executor.

It is important to name an executor who is qualified to act and who can be expected to do so. If none of those you name are legally qualified and willing to act, an administrator will be chosen from a list of family members provided by law. If there is no one on the list who will act, a public administrator usually acts for the estate. You should avoid having your estate handled by a public official who knows nothing about your property or the people who will get it.

Whether you should choose an individual or a bank or trust company (or a combination of the two) to act as executor depends on a number of factors.* You should find out in advance whether the executor you choose is willing to act. Family members and friends who will undertake the job usually will agree to do so in advance. Banks and other professionals who must maintain a more businesslike point of view often will not agree to act in advance, because so much may depend on the actual state of affairs at the time of your death. For example, a bank may be unwilling to act as executor for very small estates. When you make your will, you may have substantially more than the bank's minimum size estate. But that is no assurance that you won't spend it or lose it, leaving only a small estate.

Even though the bank will not commit itself in advance, it should be consulted before being named as executor. This will lead to a review of your will by the bank's trust department, as the bank will be con-

*These factors are discussed in chapter 19, pp. 270–71.

cerned that your directions are clear and that it is given the powers it needs to act effectively in handling your estate. The bank also may insist that you include a provision for a minimum fee for the bank, if it views the minimum provided by law as too low.

Should you name your lawyer as executor? If he or she is willing to act as his or her own lawyer without charging a second fee, this arrangement is less expensive than having an executor who is not a lawyer and must employ one.

Since the executor you name may be unwilling or unable to act after your death, or if an individual, may also be dead then, you should name one or more alternate executors.

Who will be the lawyer for your executor? Banks usually do not use their own attorneys to handle estates when they are executor. If you name a bank or trust company, it probably will hire the lawyer who drew your will. This practice often makes a great deal of sense. Your lawyer probably knows you and your family situation and the problems the will had to deal with. It makes less sense, however, if the years have passed and the lawyer who drew your will no longer is in touch with you or your affairs.

If your executor is an individual, you may want to recommend a lawyer to him or her. Some lawyers attempt to bolster their claim to represent the executor by including a direction to hire them in the will. Generally this direction does not have to be followed. In any event, it is better not to try to bind your executor in the matter but rather to leave him or her free to exercise an informed judgment in the light of the actual circumstances after your death.

173

Appoint Guardians for Your Minor Children

One of the most important reasons why any woman who has minor children or who may have them at the time she dies should make a will is to name guardians for her children. If their father survives her, no guardian will be needed while he is living, because he will be entitled to custody and also is likely to be appointed by the court as guardian of their estates, if they have any. Even if their father is living, she should name a guardian to provide for the possibility that he will die before she does.

If a woman has remarried and has minor children from a previous marriage, she may wish to name her husband as guardian, depending on his relationship with them.

Guardians are needed for minor children who have no surviving parent to take custody of them and to manage their property. A "guardian of the person" does the first and a "guardian of the estate" does the second. The same person can be both and it is usually possible to name joint guardians, which would be a reasonable arrangement if the person you want as guardian is married.

Many people name guardians without first consulting the person they have chosen, believing that they probably won't die until their children are of age and a guardian is no longer needed or that the named guardian might refuse if asked ahead of time but would rise to the occasion if need be. This is risky, and an advance understanding is much better. Even with such an understanding, alternates should be named in case the first guardian also dies or does not want to take on the responsibility when the time comes.

You should check with your lawyer to be sure that the guardians you choose are qualified to act in your state. Some states disqualify nonresidents, for example.

Exercising a Power of Appointment by Will

You may have a power of appointment—the power to dispose of property that you do not own—under the terms of a trust set up by your husband or a member of your own family. If you are a widow and your husband died before 1982, leaving a trust for you, it is likely that you have such a power.

EXAMPLE: Louise's husband's will provided a trust "to pay the income to my wife Louise for her life and on her death to pay the principal to such persons (or her estate) as my wife shall appoint by her will. If she does not make any appointment, the principal shall be paid to my descendants who survive my wife, per stirpes."

This arrangement gives Louise control over the trust property even though she does not own it. She can choose the persons to whom the trust principal shall be paid on her death and the amounts they shall receive. If she does not make any such choice, the principal will be paid in fixed shares to her husband's descendants who survive her. If Louise does not want to exercise her power, she should say so specifically in order to remove any doubt about the matter.

What Is Needed for a Valid Will

In order to make a valid will, you must have reached the minimum age under state law—usually eighteen—and be of sound mind. State law usually requires only two witnesses, but often a third is used as well, in case the others move away or are otherwise unable to testify after your death. Many states now provide for an affidavit to be signed by the witnesses when a will is executed. This affidavit means that the witnesses' testimony will not be needed to establish that they were present when the will was signed and that they believed the testator was legally competent to make a will. The witnesses must not be given anything in the will, except in states that have changed this rule.

Wills sometimes are contested on the ground that the testator made the will as a result of fraud or undue influence. The classic situation is one in which an elderly person becomes very dependent on someone and executes a will leaving most or all of the estate to that person. Sometimes these attacks are successful, and the will is held to be invalid.

To guard against an attack on these grounds, or on the ground that the testator lacked the mental capacity to make a will, a clause may be included providing that if any individuals named in the will try to upset it, they will lose their legacies. The reason for contesting a will normally is that the contestant would take a larger share if it were invalid and the estate passed under either a prior will or the intestacy law. In effect, the testator says to the legatee:

"You may have $10,000 if you accept the provisions of my will. If you contest it and succeed, you may take more. But if you fail, you will take nothing." Provisions of this type are invalid in some states because they are thought to keep the truth from coming out in a will contest.

What Your Will Cannot Do for You

There are certain things your will cannot do for you. In particular, your will cannot:

1. Avoid probate of your estate
2. Keep your husband from claiming the minimum share provided for him under state law
3. Dispose of someone else's property without his or her consent, unless you have a power of appointment over that property that can be exercised by your will

Avoid Probate

Probate is the formal process by which property that is in your name when you die is disposed of, so that debts, taxes, and administration expenses are paid and what is left is divided according to your will and state law. Many people would like to save the expense that is incurred when property goes through probate. In order for your property to avoid probate, it must either be real estate (in those states where real estate passes directly to the people named in a will, without having to be transferred by the executor) or must be in someone else's name (or in joint names with survivorship) when you die. A will cannot keep property you own when you die from going through probate.

One common way to avoid probate is for the owner to transfer property to the trustee of a revocable trust, so that the property is in the trustee's name when the owner dies. This does not save estate taxes, even though it avoids probate, because the owner can revoke the trust and take the property back. But it may have other advantages in a given case.* On the other hand, there may be income tax advantages in having property pass under your will. Your lawyer can advise you whether it makes sense to have property pass under your will for this reason.

Disinherit Your Husband

Your will cannot disinherit your husband, to the extent of the minimum share provided for him by state law. You can require him to choose between that minimum share and the provisions for him in your will. If you want to keep him from disrupting your plan after you die, you should consider the steps suggested in chapter 3, pages 66–68.

Dispose of Property You Don't Own

Your will cannot dispose of property you do not own unless you have a power of appointment over it, as described on page 23, or unless the owner accepts your disposition of his or her property. This situation comes up most often in community property states with so-called widow's election wills. The

---

* See chapter 11.

Library of Congress Catalog in Publication Data

Westfall, David, 1927–
   Every woman's guide to financial planning.

   Includes index.
     1.   Estate planning—United States.   2.   Women—
United States—Finance, Personal.   I.   Title.
KF750.W47   1984   346.7305′2   83–45259
ISBN 0–465–02120–4   347.30652

EVERY WOMAN'S GUIDE TO FINANCIAL PLANNING

DAVID WESTFALL

Basic Books, Inc., Publishers   *New York*

classic case is that of a husband whose will undertakes to dispose of both his and his wife's interest in community property, usually by placing both halves in trust to pay the income to her for life, then on her death to go to their children. The wife may, if she wishes, ignore the will and keep her half of the community property. But if she wants the income from her husband's half under the terms of his will, she must accept his disposition of her half of the community property. He has made that a condition of his gift to her.

At one time, the widow's election appeared to offer tax savings but at present there are too many tax problems to use it.

What Is Included in a Will

Usually a will begins by naming the testator and where he or she lives and by revoking all prior wills, in order to establish clearly that they are superseded by the new will. After that, the most important provisions include some or all of the following, depending on what the testator has and what he or she wants to do with it:

1. Provisions for payment of debts, taxes, and expenses of administration
2. Bequests of personal property
   a. Specific items, such as "my diamond necklace"
   b. Tangible personal property generally
   c. Cash legacies—"$25,000 to my niece"

      d. Corporate securities and other business interests—
        "my stock in Smith & Co."
   3. Devises of real estate
      a. Specific parcels—"my house and land on Shady
        Lane, Scarsdale, New York"
      b. Real estate generally—"all real estate that I may
        own at my death"
   4. Residuary bequests—"so much of my estate as is not
      disposed of by the preceding provisions hereof, I give
      and devise to my daughter Mary"
   5. Appointment of executors, trustees, and guardians,
      and provisions to give them powers to do their jobs

Lawyers refer to a "bequest" of personal property and a "devise" of real estate. Some of the bequests and devises may be in trust.*

Each provision should be written with the possibility in mind that there may not be enough property in your estate to carry out all of the provisions of your will, and that some of the people you name may die before you do. To cover the latter possibility, you can either name an alternate taker or provide that the gift shall lapse and be disposed of as part of the residue of your estate.

Payment of Debts, Taxes, and Expenses of Administration

It may seem unnecessary to provide for paying these items, when a major purpose of probate administration is to insure that they will be paid. The reason for dealing with them in your will is to direct which part of the estate will bear the burden. For

*Testamentary trusts are discussed in chapter 12.

example, if your will says nothing about payment of estate taxes, in many states the tax then is charged pro rata against the shares of all the people who receive property that is taxed when you die. If you do not want that to happen, you should direct that the tax shall be paid from a particular part of your estate.

If your estate tax may be increased because your taxable estate will include property you do not own, such as property over which you have a general power of appointment, special care is needed to deal with payment of the increased tax which results from that property being included. Your lawyer can advise you how this should be handled.

Bequests of Personal Property

Specific Items. A major problem with bequests of tangible items, such as furniture and jewelry, is to identify them properly. Some women have a highly detailed idea of where each piece of furniture or jewelry should go. A substantial amount of effort may be required to describe each item accurately. Sometimes the will may refer to a list to be prepared later, in order to permit the directions for these items to be changed from time to time without making a new will. However, in many states such a list will not be legally binding because it is not witnessed with the formalities required for the will itself.

Even if the list is not legally binding, it may be useful as an expression of your desires as to where your property should go. For example, you may give your executor the power to distribute your furniture and personal effects to anyone except himself or herself. A list can then guide your executor in exercising this power.

Tangible Personal Property Generally.

EXAMPLE: "I bequeath all of my tangible personal property, including furniture, clothing, automobiles and their equipment, and articles of personal or household use or ornament, to my husband, TOM M. JONES, if he survives me by thirty (30) days, or if he does not so survive me, to my children who so survive me in equal shares."

Requiring someone to survive for some period of time in order to receive property from your estate may be desirable to avoid having property pass through his or her estate if he or she survives for only a short time. For example, you and your husband may die in an automobile accident.

If your children are minors, the will should give your executor authority to handle their shares of tangible personal property in other ways besides requiring formal delivery to a guardian. One alternative would be to give your executor the power to deliver the children's shares to any person they are living with.

Cash Legacies.

EXAMPLE: "I give to my niece Mary if she survives me by 30 days, $25,000 or 10% of my estate, whichever is less."

Sometimes it may be desirable to limit the amount of a cash legacy so that it will not exceed a specified percentage of the estate, in order to keep from using up the residue, which usually goes to the people you are most interested in.

Corporate Securities and Other Business Interests.
EXAMPLE: "I bequeath to my daughter Mary all the stock in Smith & Co. that I may own at my death."

The problem with a bequest of this kind is that the business may be merged or bought out, or converted into a partnership, between the time the will is drawn and your death. To guard against these possibilities, the bequest should be expanded to cover property acquired as a result of these changes, if that is what you want.

Devises of Real Estate

EXAMPLE: "I devise to my daughter Jennie, if she survives me by thirty (30) days, my house and land on Shady Lane, Scarsdale, New York."

If you wish to make such a devise, you should consider what is to happen if the house is sold during your lifetime. Do you want to include an alternative bequest of money?

Residuary Bequests

EXAMPLE: "So much of my estate as is not disposed of by the preceding provisions hereof, I give and devise to my daughter Mary, if she survives me by thirty (30) days."

If the gift is in shares for two or more legatees, you should indicate clearly what is to be done with the share of one who dies during your life or who fails to survive the specified period after your death.

Suppose You Want to Change Your Will

You should review your will from time to time to be sure it continues to reflect what you want done with your property as your situation changes over the years.* If you find that you want to change your will, your lawyer should prepare either a codicil or a new will. A codicil is an amendment of an existing will. Formerly, codicils were used more often than they are today, to save typing and proofreading time. With the increased use of word processing, there will be less reason to use a codicil.

Codicils have the disadvantage of making a public record of any changes in your will. Both the will and the codicil must be filed in the public records of the probate court. A legatee may be unhappy to learn that his or her legacy was cut down, or even eliminated, from an earlier will, by a later codicil. On the other hand, it sometimes is desirable to use a codicil for the very purpose of showing clearly the extent to which an old will was changed. For example, in certain cases a change in the law will not apply to old wills unless they are changed beyond a certain degree. This was true of the generation-skipping transfer tax when it was first enacted in 1976.

---

*For a discussion of when to review your will, see chapter 20.

CHAPTER 11

What a Revocable Trust Can—and Cannot—Do for You

A REVOCABLE ("living") trust is not a substitute for a will, but it may do things for you that a will cannot do. You may set up the trust by signing an agreement with the trustee and transferring a small amount of money—$10 will do—to be held by the trustee as you have directed in the trust agreement. If you transfer only a small amount of money, you have an "unfunded" trust during your life, which you may add to by your will. If you transfer more money or property, you have a "funded" trust. The trust then provides an arrangement to handle the trust property while you are living, as well as serving the various purposes that an unfunded trust may serve.

Unfunded Revocable Trusts

An unfunded revocable trust does not "avoid probate" for property that is not in the trust when you die, except for life insurance and death benefits that you make payable to the trustee. If your property remains in your name when you die, it will have to be handled as part of your probate estate. Your will may "pour over" property from your probate estate to your revocable trust. To do this, you make the revocable trust a legatee under your will by making a bequest to the trustee.

Unfunded revocable trusts may be used for the following purposes:

1. To provide for the possibility that you will become incapacitated and will want to turn over the management of all or part of your property to the trustee
2. To avoid making the trust provisions a matter of public record
3. To avoid setting up a "court" trust that will be required to file accounts in court for approval by the judge
4. To receive proceeds of insurance on your life and death benefits payable by your employer or under a retirement arrangement you have set up

To Provide for Your Incapacity

If you become incapacitated, you probably will want to turn over the management of part or all of your property to someone else. You can use an unfunded revocable trust as a "standby" arrangement to provide for the possibility that this may happen. The trust can then be used whenever the need arises. If your health is failing, you should not wait until you have become incapacitated to set up the trust, as this process will require conferences with your lawyer as well as time in which to prepare the trust agreement.

After the trust agreement has been signed, it will be a simple matter to transfer your property to the trust whenever you want to. It may even be possible to give someone a durable power of attorney with authority to do this for you, in case you suddenly become too disabled to make the transfer yourself.

To Avoid Making the Provisions a Matter of Public Record

Whatever you include in your will becomes a matter of public record, open to anyone who takes the trouble to go to the courthouse to look it up. If you are a prominent public figure, your will may even be written up in *Trusts & Estates* magazine as the "Will of the Month." I have a file folder of these write-ups of wills of famous people. Some of them go into great detail as to how the estate was divided. Other write-ups, however, do not contain much information, because the will merely added property to a trust set up before the person died and the terms of that trust are not made public. (If your will creates a trust and the trustee files accounts in court, anyone can examine them and determine how much is paid to each beneficiary.)

Of course, using a revocable trust, with a pour over from your will, does not guarantee complete secrecy for your arrangements for your property. If the trust owns real estate, it may be necessary to record the trust agreement in the public land records in order to have a clear title to the property. And even if it does not own real estate, copies of the trust agreement are likely to be on file in a number of places—the trustee's office, the office of the trustee's lawyer, the Internal Revenue Service, and perhaps the offices of various stock transfer agents as well. But even if it is on file in all of these places, it will not be anywhere near as much in public view as your will down at the courthouse.

You may feel there is no reason to keep the provisions of your will secret. In that case, this reason for using a revocable trust does not apply to you.

To Avoid the Creation of a Court Trust

In some states, trusts created by will are "court" trusts, but a trust created during your life is not a court trust even if you add to it by your will. The trustees of a court trust must qualify in the probate court and often must file accounts periodically for approval by the judge. This is an additional expense for the trust, particularly if the court must appoint a "guardian ad litem" to go over the accounts for any interested parties who are minors or whose interests cannot be determined when the account is filed because, for example, they are unborn.

In some states, appointment of guardians ad litem is treated as a form of political patronage. Your trust may have to pay them big fees for their work. If this is true in your state, it may be an important reason to avoid creating a trust in your will and to use a revocable trust which you add to by your will instead.

To Receive Proceeds of Insurance on Your Life and Death Benefits

Life insurance and death benefits under a plan set up by your employer, or under your own retirement arrangement, often may be made payable to the trustee of a trust. If the insurance or death benefit is payable to your executor, it will be treated as part of your probate estate. This will increase the cost of handling your estate. Making the amount payable to an unfunded revocable trust may reduce expenses by "avoiding probate" and in the case of a death benefit, may also save estate tax.* It also frees the amount from claims of creditors of your estate.

Funded Revocable Trusts

A funded revocable trust is one to which you transfer more than a small amount of money during your life, so that title to the property transferred is in the name of the trustee when you die. Funded revocable trusts may be used for the following purposes:

1. To avoid probate, *possibly* reducing the total cost of carrying out your personal financial plan
2. To provide an arrangement for the management of your property if you are incapacitated or simply wish to turn the job over to someone else
3. To avoid interruptions and delays in the management of your property when you die

*See chapter 15, p. 235.

4. To make the law of a state other than the state you live in apply to the trust
5. To choose a trustee who may not be allowed to act as trustee under your will

To Avoid Probate

Whether the use of a funded revocable trust will reduce the total cost of carrying out your personal financial plan depends on so many factors that there is no general rule to go by. However, the following items should be taken into account:

- How will use of the trust affect the commissions charged by your executor and the fee of the lawyer for your estate?

Executors' commissions usually are based on a percentage of the value of the estate, with the percentage dropping as the value goes up. Commissions may be set either by law or by the practice of banks and trust companies in your area. Some banks clearly do not include property in a funded revocable trust in figuring their commissions; others include such property, or a portion of its value. Of course, if a family member or friend will act as executor and charge no fee, executors' commissions won't be in the picture at all. However, an executor who is not a professional is likely to require more paid professional assistance in doing the job.

The fee of the lawyer for an estate may be based either on a similar sliding scale percentage of the value of the estate or on time spent. If the fee is based on time, use of a funded revocable trust may not result in any significant reduction, as the lawyer's responsibilities will include listing the trust assets for federal and state estate and inheritance tax purposes just as if you had created no trust.

- How will use of the trust affect your lawyer's fees for preparing the documents required to carry out your personal financial plan?

If your lawyer must draft a revocable trust agreement—whether or not it is funded during your lifetime—in addition to a will, more work will be required than if you use a will alone.

- What will be the fees of the trustee during your life, as compared to the cost of getting help in managing the trust property from another source?
- What will be the effect on income taxes after your death, if your property is in a funded revocable trust when you die rather than passing through your estate?

Your lawyer can advise you as to how these factors are likely to add up in your own case.

To Provide an Arrangement for Managing Your Property

A funded revocable trust allows the trustee to manage your property for your benefit while you live. Although other arrangements, such as a durable power of attorney,* may be used, depending on the law of your state, a funded revocable trust gives you greater protection and is more likely to be accepted by other people who deal with the trustee.

*See chapter 2, pp. 41–42.

To Avoid Interruptions and Delays when You Die

Your death freezes any property that is in your name until either an executor named in your will or an administrator appointed by the court has qualified to act in dealing with it. How soon this can happen depends greatly on state law. There have been efforts to simplify and shorten the procedure, but it still takes some time. Meanwhile, no one can sell anything that is in your name.

If your property is in a trust when you die, the trustee will be able to act without delay if a sale is deemed advisable. How important this is depends on the nature of your property.

To Choose the State Law that will Apply to Your Trust

Generally, property disposed of by your will is controlled by the law of the state where you live, except for real estate in other states, which is controlled by the law of the state where it is located. Sometimes you may prefer to have the law of another state apply. For example, your home state may give your husband the right to claim a minimum share of your estate, including any trust that you have power to revoke. Another state may not include revocable trusts in computing your husband's forced share and may apply its rule to trusts created in the state during your life, even though you are not a resident of the state when you die. In that case, creating a funded revocable trust in another state during your life might reduce the minimum share your husband could take.

To Choose a Trustee in Another State

Many states do not allow banks and trust companies incorporated in other states to act as trustees under wills of residents. Thus, if you move to another state and wish to have the institution you were familiar with in your old state act as trustee after you die, it may be necessary to set up a funded revocable trust in order to accomplish this.

CHAPTER 12

How to Use Trusts to Dispose of Property

ANY IRREVOCABLE TRUST you create during your life nearly always is set up to save taxes. This is *not* true of trusts of property that you own when you die, which may be set up for either tax or nontax reasons. As discussed in chapters 10 and 11, the trust may be a trust created under your will or a *revocable* trust created during your life. The trust may be used to qualify for the federal estate tax deduction for property passing to your husband. But it also may accomplish goals that have nothing to do with taxes and that cannot be accomplished in any other way.

After your death, no one except a trustee can step into your shoes and make the same decisions about who is to enjoy your money that you could make while you lived. In effect, you give the trustee directions in your will or revocable trust agreement: "This is how I would handle my money if I were living. Now I can't do it myself any more, so you do it for me." You can give the trustee specific directions as to how much income and principal is to be paid to each beneficiary, or you can lay down general guidelines to help the trustee use the same judgment you would have used.

The ways in which trusts may be useful to you in disposing of your property after your death depend on the amount of property you have and on what you would like to do with it. The kinds of trusts that are most likely to be useful to women who have a limited amount of property and are mainly concerned with providing support for a husband or dependant parent or child, are discussed in the first section of this chapter. The remainder of the chapter deals with the kinds of trusts that are more likely to be useful to women with a substantial amount of property, who want to save estate taxes and to set up a long-term arrangement to provide for their grandchildren and possibly great-grandchildren.

If You Have Only a Limited Amount of Property

Let's take the case of Sarah, a married woman with an estate that is not large enough to be subject to the federal estate tax. Sarah's husband is retired, and she uses part of her income to help meet the family expenses. She also helps support her mother, whose living expenses are more than she gets from Social Security. Sarah's children are grown and self-supporting.

Sarah wants to provide her mother with the income she needs to live on, and she wants the balance to go to her husband. If either her mother or her husband needs principal in addition to cover living expenses, Sarah wants them to have that as well.

Sarah could simply divide her property between her mother and her husband and give each a share directly, without using a trust. But if she does this, she may give either her mother or her husband more or less than is actually needed for support. Furthermore, some of the money that is needed for support of one of them may end up in the hands of other people.

For example, suppose Sarah left half of her estate to her mother, who died shortly afterward. The money from Sarah would then pass under her mother's will, or under the intestacy laws if her mother left no will. Sarah's money could easily end up in the hands of her brothers and sisters and children, when it is her husband who needs it to live on.

Suppose Sarah leaves the other half of her estate to her husband and he remarries. If he then is divorced or dies and his second wife survives him, Sarah's money may end up in the hands of the second wife, when Sarah's mother needs it to live on.

If Sarah left her money in trust for her mother and her husband, instead of directly to them, the trustee could be given authority to use income and principal as needed for their support as long as they lived. After they both had died, whatever was left could go to Sarah's children or grandchildren. This arrangement would give Sarah's money to the people she would have given it to were she alive.

If You Have a Substantial Amount of Property

Let's use as our example, Louise, a well-to-do grandmother. Her husband, George, is living and also is well off, although he does not have as much money as Louise.

Louise is mainly concerned with providing for her children, Jennie and Mark, and for Jennie's children. She is willing to make a gift to George to whatever extent necessary to save estate taxes.* If she wants to use trusts to make her gifts, she has several alternatives both for George's gift and for her gifts to the children and grandchildren.

These trusts all offer important advantages over Louise's other alternative, which is to give property directly to George, Jennie, and Mark, and assume that in due course it will go to Jennie's children.

If Louise wants to make a gift to a charity, she should consider the tax advantages offered by charitable split-interest trusts.†

*See chapter 15, pp. 233–35.
†See pp. 203–204.

Marital Deduction Trusts

To save estate taxes by getting a marital deduction, Louise need not create a trust. The deduction is allowed if she leaves property directly to George. But if she follows this latter route, she loses control over the property, and it may never reach her children or grandchildren. Even if Louise has confidence that George won't spend it, there are other risks to consider.

George may remarry after Louise dies and then be divorced. In many states, if George is divorced, the judge can assign any of his property to his ex-wife, including that which came from Louise. If George dies, leaving his second wife as his widow, in most states she can claim a share of his estate, without regard to the terms of his will. Again, this includes the part of his estate that came from Louise.

A marital deduction trust can minimize the risk that Louise's property would end up with George's second wife, either after his death or after a divorce. It can also be used to protect the property from his creditors, or to minimize his income taxes after Louise dies.

The major kinds of marital deduction trusts that Louise can use to save estate taxes are:

1. A power of appointment trust (George must get all of the income for life and have the power to dispose of the principal when he dies)
2. A qualified terminable interest trust (George must get all of the income for life but need not have any power over the principal)
3. An estate trust (George need not get income, but the principal and all income that is not paid to George must be paid to his estate when he dies)

4. A qualified charitable remainder trust (George must get either an annuity or a percentage of principal each year for life, and on his death, the trust must go to a charity)

Power of Appointment Trust. For many years, the power of appointment trust was the most common way to get the federal estate tax marital deduction for a trust. It has two serious disadvantages if Louise wants to limit George's control over her property: George must get all of the trust income for his life; and he must have power to dispose of the principal by his will to anyone, including his own estate. The only advantage of the power of appointment trust, as compared to a direct gift, in limiting George's control over the property is that he can't spend principal during his life unless Louise says so when she sets up the trust.

Qualified Terminable Interest Trust. The Qualified Terminable Interest Property (QTIP) trust was added to the tax law by the Economic Recovery Tax Act of 1981. Many people are using it because it allows them to get the marital deduction without giving their spouses control over principal. If Louise sets up a QTIP trust, all George has to get is the income from the trust property for his life. On his death, it can pass to Louise's children or can continue in trust for their benefit, or it can go to whomever she chooses.

Louise may allow principal to be paid to George and may give him some control over the trust when he dies, if she wants to. For example, he could have the power to change the children's shares by his will.

Estate Trust. Very few people use the estate trust. It requires that if any income is paid out, it must go to George, and the accumulated income and principal must be paid to his estate when he dies. Using an estate trust allows Louise to get the marital deduction without having trust income paid and taxed to George, which is an advantage if he is in a high income tax bracket. But it leaves him with control when he dies over both the accumulated income and the trust principal.

Qualified Charitable Remainder Trust. A qualified charitable remainder trust allows Louise to combine a gift of a life income to George with a gift of the principal (and any accumulated income) to a charity when he dies. His life income must be either a fixed amount of money each year (an annuity) or a percentage of the current value of the principal each year.

If the trust provides an annuity for George, it must be at least 5 percent of the value of the principal when the trust is set up. If the amount paid to George is based on the current value of the principal, it is technically a "unitrust amount" and must be at least 5 percent of the value of the principal, or the trust income for the year, whichever is less.

Louise's estate will get a marital deduction for the value of George's interest and a charitable deduction for the charity's gift. Together these two deductions will be equal to the full value of the property in the trust.

Trusts for Children and Grandchildren

While Louise is living, she doesn't need a trust to make gifts to her children and grandchildren because she is around to make the gifts herself. She can decide from year to year or month to month who needs income to spend or a loan to make a down payment on a house or money for college tuition or medical expenses. If Louise sets up a trust during her life to make her gifts for her, it is usually in order to make the gifts at a lower tax cost.

When Louise has died, only a trustee can step in and make the same kinds of judgments she would make if she were living, as to which child or grandchild needs and deserves help from her, and in what amount.

Many women in Louise's situation have left their property directly to their children, rather than in trust. This arrangement may make sense for any of several reasons. First of all, the amount involved may not be large enough to justify the trouble and expense of leaving it in trust. Even if it is large enough, the woman may have confidence that her children will handle the property the way she would have, or she may simply prefer to let her children do what they want with her money.

Louise, however, may decide that none of these reasons for leaving property directly to children apply in her case, and that she would prefer to leave her property in trust instead. There are two major advantages of doing so.

The trustee is in a better position to handle the property in the way Louise herself would have. That is, the trustee does not have any personal temptation to spend Louise's money (unless her will or trust agreement specifically allows this), and as trustee, is under a legal obligation to follow Louise's directions.

The second advantage of leaving the property in trust is that the trust offers protection. Property that is left directly to Louise's children is exposed to the claims of their spouses and creditors and may be taxed more heavily than property that is left in trust for them instead.

The reason a trust offers so much protection is that for purposes of taxes, rights of spouses, and rights of creditors, the law makes a sharp distinction between property you own and property of a trust set up by someone else from which you receive money or property. This is true even though you may have many of the rights to the trust property that an owner would have.

If the trust is created by Louise's will, it may continue for as long as she wants, up to twenty-one years after the death of someone who is living when Louise dies. If the trust is created during her life but is revocable until her death, the time limit should be the same, although the law may not be clear on this point in some states.

The major kinds of long-term trusts that Louise might set up for her children and grandchildren on her death are the same as during her life:*

1. A nondiscretionary trust, in which Jennie, Mark, and the grandchildren are given fixed rights to income and principal
2. A trust with powers of appointment or beneficiary powers, in which, for example, Jennie may be given various powers to withdraw principal for herself or to give it to her children

---

*See chapter 8, pp. 140–47, for a more detailed discussion of the various kinds of long-term trusts.

3. A discretionary trust, with powers given to a trustee to decide who gets income and principal, and how much

In setting up a trust to dispose of property upon her death Louise has greater freedom, because there no longer is any possibility that she will be treated as owner for tax purposes and taxed on the trust income. Depending on who is named as trustee, however, it may still be necessary to limit the trustee's powers, in order to protect her children and grandchildren from unnecessary taxes.*

Charitable Split-Interest Trusts

If Louise wants to leave property to a charity, there may be important tax advantages in combining the charity's gift with provisions for her descendants. If she wants to do this, her major alternatives are the same as during her life,† except that she can no longer benefit from the trust herself:

1. A charitable remainder trust, in which her daughter Jennie or one or more other members of Louise's family receive payments for their lives or for a period of years. After that time, the charity gets the principal and any accumulated income.
2. A charitable lead trust, in which the charity's interest comes first and is followed by provisions for members of Louise's family.

Setting up a charitable remainder trust when she dies gives Louise no income tax deduction, unlike

---

* See chapters 16 and 17.
† See chapter 8, pp. 147–51.

one set up during her life.* However, the trust itself is generally exempt from income taxes, no matter when it is set up. This means that if it realizes a gain from the sale of stock, there is no tax on the gain, even though the money the trust receives from the sale will be used as long as Jennie lives to produce income to make payments to her. If the trust's income is more than those payments, it pays no tax on the accumulated income, because any accumulation on hand when Jennie dies will go to charity. Jennie will pay income tax on the payments she receives from the trust, to the extent they represent income or capital gains of the trust.

Both kinds of charitable split-interest trusts provide estate tax savings if set up when Louise dies, like the gift tax savings if the trust is set up during her life.†

Who Should Be Trustee

In choosing trustees, Louise should bear in mind that the tax rules create problems for a trustee who has the power to pay income or principal to himself or herself or to support dependants. Louise can avoid these rules in one of two ways. She can limit the trustee's powers and have whomever she wants as trustee. Or she can give the powers she wants to a trustee who is not caught by these tax rules.

In addition to deciding how to avoid these tax problems, Louise also needs to take into account

---

*See chapter 8, p. 149.
†See chapter 8, pp. 149–51.

nontax factors in her choice of trustees. These factors are the same as for trusts she sets up during her life.*

What Property Should Be Transferred to Which Trust

Property in any form of marital deduction trust for George will be included in figuring his estate tax when he dies. So from a tax standpoint, property that is likely to go up a lot in value should be left to the trust for Louise's descendants, rather than the trust for George, as long as there is enough other property to make his trust as large as she wants it to be.

*See chapter 19, pp. 270–76.

PART V

HOW TO SAVE
TAXES YOURSELF

NOTHING *is certain but death and taxes,'' wrote Benjamin Franklin, almost two hundred years ago. Ever since then, many people have been handicapped by the idea that taxes, like death, are beyond human control. Nothing could be farther from the truth. People who are willing and able to take taxes into account when they make their personal financial plans may be able to reduce substantially—and sometimes even cut out completely—federal income, gift, estate, and generation-skipping transfer taxes.*

Tax savings may carry a price, but often that price is less than you expect. Often a plan that saves taxes does not require any major change in the way you would have disposed of your income and property if the taxes involved did not exist. And even if major changes in your plan are required, the amount saved may be large enough to make it worth modifying a plan based solely on your personal preferences.

Saving taxes doesn't stop at one's death. You may be able to minimize tax burdens for members of your family by the way you provide for them.* This part deals with saving taxes yourself during your life and on your death: income taxes (chapter 13), gift taxes (chapter 14), and estate and inheritance taxes (chapter 15).

---

*The relevant strategies are covered in part 6.

How to Save Income Taxes

THIS CHAPTER shows how you can save income taxes during your lifetime. You can use any of a number of tools:

1. Direct gifts
2. Trust gifts
3. Interest-free loans
4. Charitable contributions

You can also use retirement arrangements that you set up, and you may be able to set up a tax-deferred annuity arrangement with your employer.* Either kind allows income taxes to be postponed until the money is paid to you or to your beneficiary after

---

*See chapter 2, pp. 36–37, for a discussion of tax-deferred annuity arrangements.

your death. In the meantime, you get the benefit of an interest-free loan from the Treasury, because the money in the retirement arrangement is invested for you without any income tax being deducted.

Sometimes you can also save income taxes by doing nothing. For example, you can hold on to property that has gone up in price, instead of selling it and having to pay income tax on a capital gain. After your death, whoever receives the property will have a new basis to use as the cost in figuring gain or loss when it is sold. The new basis generally is the value of the property at your death (or on the alternate valuation date used for the estate tax, if your executor elects to use that date). What it means is that the gain reflecting the increase in value during your life is never subject to income tax.

The new basis generally applies to whatever you own, with the exception of property someone gives you within the year before your death. If that person gets the property back from your estate, he or she keeps the old basis. For example, if your husband gives you stock worth $10,000 which cost him $2,000 and you die within the year, leaving either the stock or proceeds from its sale to him, the basis for the stock is still $2,000.

If you and your husband live in a community property state, when one of you dies, both halves of the community property get a new basis, even though only one half is included in the taxable estate of whoever died first.

If you and your husband have property in joint names as joint tenants or tenants by the entirety and one of you dies, only half of the property gets a new basis. For this reason, holding property with your husband in either of these ways may be expensive if the property is worth more than you paid for it. If you survive your husband, you may have a large taxable gain when you sell, on the half that did not get a new basis when he died.

If the property was in your husband's name alone, it would all get a new basis for income tax. This is true even though there is no federal estate tax on it, because the property would be treated as a marital deduction gift to you, the surviving spouse. The same would be true if the property were in your name alone and you died first. Of course, it isn't always clear ahead of time which spouse will be the first to die. But from an income tax standpoint, if the property is worth more than it cost, ideally it should be in the name of that spouse.

Direct Gifts

Let's go back to Louise again and assume she has enough income to be taxed in the top 50 percent bracket. Of course, that bracket applies only to part of her income. She starts at the bottom rate, like everyone else. But if a gift of income-producing property can shift income from her top bracket, where she pays 50 cents on the dollar, to an individual who is in only an 11 percent bracket, there is a saving of 39 cents on each dollar shifted. As more income is shifted, the saving drops if Louise's top rate goes down and the top rate of the person to whom income is shifted builds up. But the total saved still may be large.

After you make a gift of property, the income it produces is taxable to the recipient and not to you, the donor. For example, if Louise gives her daughter a bond, the interest that accrues after the gift is made is taxable income of the daughter. But interest that accrues before Louise makes the gift is taxable to Louise, even if her daughter collects it. This is because the interest that has already accrued when Louise makes the gift is income to her whenever it is paid. It cannot be assigned for tax purposes to anyone else.

You cannot use a gift of your earnings to shift income for tax purposes. For example, if Louise has a business or profession and she transfers the right to collect the bills for her services to someone else, she is still taxed when the bills are collected.

Trust Gifts

Trust gifts have been used so often to save income taxes that Congress has laid down ground rules as to which trusts work for this purpose and which do not. If Louise wants to use a trust gift to save income taxes by making the income taxable either to the trust or to the people who receive money or property from it, she must follow five general rules:

1. The trust must last ten years and one day or until the person who gets the trust income has died, whichever happens first.
2. Neither Louise nor anyone who is a "related or subordinate party," such as her brother or her child, can have broad powers to decide who will get the trust income and principal, or at what time.
3. Louise's power to borrow from the trust must be restricted.
4. Neither Louise nor anyone else can have the power to give her back the trust property.
5. The trustee can't be given the power to pay income to Louise or her husband or to use it to pay their bills or their life insurance premiums.

Some of these general rules have exceptions. Several potentially important exceptions are described below.

The Trust must last ten years and one day or until the person who gets the income dies. You may want to make the trust last longer than ten years because the clock doesn't start ticking until the property actually has been transferred to the trust, and because you may want to add to the trust after it has been set up. If you add property when the trust has less than ten years and one day left to go, you will be taxed on the income from the property added.

Louise, or a "related or subordinate party," cannot have broad powers to determine who will get income or principal, or at what time. The tax law contains detailed rules as to what powers Louise may have, what additional powers trustees who are defined as "related or subordinate parties" may have, and finally what powers may be given to trustees if at least one-half of them are treated as being "independent." In this last situation, the allowable powers are extremely broad for the trustees if one-half of them are legally "independent," even though Louise picked them because she thinks they will handle the trust the way she wants.

Note that "independent" here means merely in a legal sense. For example, Louise's husband is a related party but her son-in-law is not, so the two of them together are one-half independent—even if Louise picked them because she thinks they will handle the trust the way she wants. They can be given extremely broad powers without making Louise taxable on the trust income.

Your lawyer can advise you who can be trustee of your trust without causing the trust income to be taxed to you. Sometimes it is worth limiting the powers you might have wanted the trustee to have in order to be able to choose the trustee you prefer.

Louise's power to borrow from the trust must be restricted. She may borrow only if the loan is made by an independent trustee who is authorized to make loans generally, and the loan provides adequate interest and adequate security.

Neither Louise nor anyone else can have the power to give her back the trust property. She can, however, have a power to revoke the trust and take back the trust property after the minimum time described in (1) (i.e., after ten years and one day or the death of the person who gets the income).

The trustee can't be given the power to pay income to Louise or her husband or to use it to pay their bills or life insurance premiums. If, for example, the trustee had the power to pay for food for Louise, she would be taxed as owner of the trust income even though the trustee never actually bought her anything to eat. However, the trustee can be given the power to use income to support Louise's legal dependents, if she has any. The mere chance that income may be used for this purpose won't make Louise taxable on it. But she will be taxed on any income the trustee actually uses to support her dependents.

So if Louise has a minor child who she is legally obligated to support and the trustee spends trust income to buy food for the child, Louise will be taxed on that income. But if the trustee had not actually used the income for this purpose, Louise wouldn't be taxed merely because he might have.

Interest-Free Loans

Louise can use an interest-free loan to shift income to one of her children for tax purposes. The child can invest the money and earn income from it. Under present law, that income is taxable to the child, rather than Louise, even though she has the right to demand payment at any time.

Although the courts are divided as to whether a gift is made when Louise lends money without charging interest,* lenders like Louise have not been taxed on the income the child earns by investing the money.

*See chapter 9, pp. 155-58.

Charitable Gifts

Most people know that an income tax deduction is allowed for charitable gifts. What is not as well known is that you can get extra income tax savings if the gift is made in property, rather than money.

Three kinds of gifts offer special tax savings:

1. A gift of property that has gone up in value, so that you would be taxed on a gain if you sold it instead of making the gift
2. A gift of your home or farm which will cause the property to pass to a charity after you or members of your family die
3. A gift to a charitable split-interest trust[†]

How can you be sure your charitable gift is being used effectively? Some charitable organizations spend unreasonably large amounts on fund raising, accumulate vast sums instead of using them to meet current needs, and benefit board members at the expense of the charitable cause they seek to promote. One effective way to get the facts is through the National Information Bureau, Inc. The Bureau is an impartial advisory service reporting on hundreds of charitable organizations. It will send you, free of charge, its "Wise Giving Guide," containing standards for charities, such as reasonable fund-raising expenses and a responsible governing board that serves without compensation. In addition, at your request, you will also be sent three reports on charities you are interested in, showing whether they satisfy

[†] See chapter 8, pp. 147–51.

the standards laid out in the guide. If you contribute $25 to the bureau, you may have as many reports as you want. The bureau's address is National Information Bureau, Inc., 419 Park Avenue South, New York, NY 10016.

A Gift of Property That Has Gone Up in Value

If you give property that has gone up in value instead of selling it and giving the money, the charity gets the same amount and you usually get the same deduction. However, you save the tax you would have paid if you had sold the property and realized a gain.

For example, suppose you bought stock for $10,000 which is now worth $50,000 and you are in the top 50 percent income tax bracket. If you sell the stock and give the proceeds to charity, you will have a deduction for your charitable gift that will save you $25,000 (if it doesn't reduce your taxable income so much that you are no longer in a 50 percent bracket).

You will also have a taxable gain of $40,000. If you held the stock for more than a year, only 40 percent of the gain is subject to tax. But even so, your federal income tax on $16,000 would be $8,000, in addition to any state or local income tax on the gain. If you gave the stock to the charity instead of selling it and giving the proceeds, your charitable deduction would still reduce your income tax by $25,000, but you would save the $8,000 tax on the gain. The charity could sell the stock and pay no tax.

If you give the charity property that is not a "capital asset," so that your gain would not have been a capital gain if you had made the sale yourself, your deduction is cut down. For example, you may give property you hold for sale to your customers, like a retailer's stock of goods. You can deduct only part of the value of a gift of this kind of property.

A Gift of a Remainder Interest in Your Home or Farm

Suppose Louise decides she would like her home to go to a charity after she dies. She can make a gift of the home while she is living, but keep the right to live there until she dies. The charity will have what lawyers call a "remainder" interest in the home and will be entitled to the property after Louise dies. If she wanted to, Louise could also give her child (or anyone she chose) the right to occupy the home for their lives.

The advantage for Louise of setting this arrangement up during her life, instead of in her will, is that she gets an income tax deduction for the value of her gift to the charity. The deduction is based on the value of the home when she makes the gift, discounted for a period equal to her life expectancy and adjusted to allow for depreciation on the building during her life. The tables the Internal Revenue Service now uses to value such gifts reflect a 10 percent rate, but this could be changed.

This arrangement can also be used for a gift of a farm, but not for tangible personal property, such as a painting. For such property, the charitable income tax deduction is not allowed until the charity is entitled to possession of the property. If that is not until Louise dies, no income tax deduction will be allowed either for her or her estate.

CHAPTER 14

How You Can Save
Gift Taxes

THE GIFT TAX is a purely voluntary tax. You can avoid it by making no gifts of more than $10,000 to any one person in any year, if your gifts are all what lawyers call a "present interest." Even if you make gifts over and above the $10,000 per person exclusion, you owe no gift tax until your gifts add up to more than the amount that is tax free because of the special credit provided by law.

This lifetime tax-free amount is $325,000 in 1984. It increases each year until 1987:

1985—$400,000
1986—$500,000
1987—$600,000

The amount applies to the total gifts over the $10,000

exclusion that you make throughout your life, beginning with 1932, when the present gift tax became law.

Let's assume, for example, that Louise makes the following outright gifts in 1984 and never made any gifts before:

To Mark	$10,000
To Jennie	350,000
TOTAL	$360,000

Of this $360,000, only $340,000 counts for gift tax purposes, because the $10,000 exclusion covers all that Louise gave to Mark and $10,000 of her gift to Jennie.

You figure your gift tax first and then deduct from the tax the special credit provided by law. Under the rate schedule provided by law, the tax in 1984 on gifts of $340,000 is $101,400. From this Louise deducts the special credit, $96,300, and pays gift tax of $5,100.

Suppose Louise made the same gifts again in 1985. Her taxable gifts that year will be $340,000, which is added to her gifts of $340,000 in 1984 to produce a lifetime total of $680,000.

The tax on gifts of $680,000 is $222,400. However, the special credit used to figure the tax on gifts made in 1985 is $121,800, leaving a balance of $100,600. Louise already paid $5,100 in 1984, so for 1985 she owes $95,500.

Assume that after making these gifts, Louise dies in 1986, owning property worth $500,000 (after deducting her debts and the expenses of administering her estate). Estate and inheritance taxes paid to the state she lived in were $60,000, which is more than the maximum credit for these taxes allowed against the federal estate tax. How will her gifts affect the tax on her estate, if she gets no deduction for property going to her husband or to charity?

Louise's taxable lifetime gifts (those above the $10,000 exclusion) made after 1976, plus gift taxes on gifts within three years of her death, are added to the property she owns when she dies. Her estate tax is figured on the total. The estate tax has the same rates and special credit as the gift tax. The result is that Louise only gets the credit once. If she uses it up with lifetime gifts, it will not actually reduce the tax on property she owns when she dies.

Louise's estate tax would be figured like this:

Taxable estate (property Louise owned when she died less her debts and expenses of administering her estate)	$ 500,000	
Gifts	680,000	
Gift taxes paid	100,600	
Total	$1,280,600	
Estate tax before credits		$461,458
Less credits:		
Special credit provided by law if you die in 1986	$ 155,800	
State death taxes	50,358	
Gift taxes paid	100,600	
Total credits	$306,758	
Estate tax payable		$154,700

Because Louise died within three years of the time

221

she made her gifts, *both* the part of the gifts over the $10,000 exclusion and the gift tax she paid are added to the property she owned when she died, to figure her estate tax. If Louise had died in 1989, more than three years after all of her gifts were made, the gifts would be added in to figure her estate tax when she died, but the gift tax would not be. Her estate tax would then be figured like this:

Taxable estate	$ 500,000	
Gifts	680,000	
Total	$1,180,000	
Estate tax before credits		$419,600
Less credits:		
Special credit provided by law if you die after 1986	$ 192,800	
State death taxes	43,920	
Gift taxes paid	100,600	
Total credits	$337,320	
Estate tax payable		$82,280

There are five major ways to save gift taxes:

1. The $10,000 per donee (recipient) exclusion, which allows you to give $10,000 apiece to as many people as you want, without having your gifts count
2. Gift-splitting with your husband, and the gift tax marital deduction for gifts to him
3. The exclusion for gifts made by paying school tuition or for medical care
4. Arranging to give property that will have a low value for gift tax purposes, compared to what it will be worth later
5. Disclaiming property you are entitled to receive from

an estate so that it passes to someone you want to help

The $10,000 Per Donee Exclusion

By far the most important way for someone like Louise to save gift taxes is the annual exclusion. This allows you to give $10,000 every year to as many people as you want, as long as the gift is a present interest, so that the donee gets rights to the property when the gift is made, rather than at some future date. If your gifts do not exceed the $10,000 per donee limit, they generally do not count for either the gift tax or the estate tax, unless the gift is insurance on your life. In that case, it still doesn't count for the gift tax, but the policy proceeds will be counted for estate tax if you die within three years of making the gift.

The $10,000 exclusion may allow Louise to transfer a large amount of property to her children and grandchildren over the years without paying any taxes. For example, if she has two children and four grandchildren, she can give each of them $10,000, or a total of $60,000 per year, right up to the time she dies.

In order to be a present interest and get the exclusion, the gift doesn't have to put the money in the donee's hands, if you make the kind of gift the law recognizes for this purpose. Chapter 8 showed the

223

variety of forms of trusts and custodianships that are treated as giving the donee a present interest.

Gift Splitting and the Gift Tax Marital Deduction

Gift splitting applies to gifts you and your husband make to third persons; the gift tax marital deduction applies to gifts one of you makes to the other.

Gift Splitting

For married women, gift splitting may double the amount they can give tax free each year. For example, if Louise wants to give her children $20,000 each and have it all covered by the $10,000 annual exclusion, her husband can consent to treat half of her gifts as if he had made them. As long as he doesn't make any gifts to the children himself, Louise's $20,000 gifts will be covered by the combination of her and her husband's $10,000 exclusions and will not count for either her gift tax or her estate tax, if the gifts do no consist of insurance on her life. If she gives insurance on her life and dies within three years, the policy proceeds will count in figuring her estate tax.

In addition to allowing use of both her and her husband's present interest exclusions, gift splitting may save gift taxes on a gift of more than $20,000, if Louise's husband is in a lower gift tax bracket than she is.

Some women have tried to combine present interest exclusions with someone other than a husband. For example, after her husband dies, Louise may want to continue to give $20,000 each to her two children. So she gives $10,000 to each child herself and gives her sister $20,000, with the understanding that she will pass the money on to Louise's children. This does not work. Louise will be treated as having used her sister as an agent to make gifts to her children, so that she has given a total of $20,000 to each of them. Only $10,000 to each child will be covered by the exclusion.

Gift Tax Marital Deduction

The gift tax marital deduction keeps gifts between Louise and her husband from counting for gift tax purposes as long as the gift is the kind the law recognizes for this purpose. Direct gifts generally are covered, as are the kinds of gifts in trust that would satisfy the requirements for the estate tax marital deduction.*

The gift tax marital deduction is useful in keeping transfers between you and your husband from being subject to gift taxes, if the amount involved is too large to be covered by the $10,000 present interest exclusion. Sometimes there is a tax advantage in making larger marital deduction gifts, in order to make your estates more nearly equal in size and hence save estate taxes.

For many women, there is no important tax reason to make lifetime gifts to a husband because they

*See chapter 15, pp. 233–35.

can leave him as much as they want when they die, free of estate tax, by using the estate tax marital deduction. However, if Louise is wealthy and her husband is not, there may be a tax advantage for her in using the gift tax marital deduction to make gifts to him during his life. If he dies before Louise does, and his taxable estate is less than the tax-free amount ($325,000 if he dies in 1984), the opportunity for him to leave the full tax-free amount to the children (or grandchildren) will have been missed. This would not have been the case had Louise made a lifetime gift to him so that his taxable estate equaled or exceeded the tax-free amount. Louise's gift can take the form of a QTIP trust,* giving her husband only income for life and providing that on his death the property shall be divided among the children. With this arrangement, her husband will not be able to leave the property to anyone else.

Making Gifts by Paying Tuition or Medical Expenses

Louise can make additional gifts to her children and grandchildren (or anyone else) that will not count against the $10,000 annual per donee exclusion by paying for their school tuition or medical expenses. In order to use this exclusion, Louise must make the payment directly to the school or to the person pro-

*See chapter 12, p. 199.

viding medical care. She cannot reimburse her child or grandchild for expenses that have already been paid.

Giving Property When It Has a Low Value

You may be able to save gift taxes by giving property that you expect to go up in value before the rise has occurred, because property is valued for gift tax purposes as of the date the gift is made. For example, if you own land that will become more valuable after a highway is constructed or a shopping center is built, the full increase in value may not be reflected in an appraisal until construction is completed. If you make your gift before then, the value for gift tax purposes may be lower than if you wait.

Disclaiming Property You Are Entitled to Receive from an Estate

One way to make a gift without being subject to gift tax is to disclaim a bequest or intestate share in someone's estate, so that it is not paid to you and goes instead to someone you want to help. For example, your mother's will may leave you a legacy of $50,000 and give the residue to your children. If you would like to help your children without making a

227

taxable gift to them, you may do so by refusing to accept the legacy and letting it pass to your children as part of the residue. In order to achieve this result, the disclaimer has to meet standards contained in the tax law.

You also may sometimes find it advantageous to disclaim a legacy from your husband. For example, he may have given you a direct bequest of $100,000 and provided that the balance of his property shall go into a trust from which you get the income only if the trustee decides you need it, with the principal going to your children when you die. If you think you may not need the $100,000, you can disclaim the legacy so that the trust will be that much larger. The trustee can give you the income if he or she decides you need it. After your death, the trust will pass to your children without another estate tax.

CHAPTER 15

How to Save Estate and Inheritance Taxes

FOR MOST PEOPLE, the federal estate tax is *not* a serious problem because their estates will not be large enough to pay the tax. But if you have enough property, the tax soon begins to bite. The effective starting rate is over 30 percent, after deducting the credit for state death taxes. If your taxable estate is $1 million, the combined federal and state death taxes may easily exceed $250,000 if you die in 1984—taking one-quarter of your property away from your family.

The reason the tax starts to bite so sharply and suddenly is that a special credit provided by law offsets the entire tax on estates of $325,000 or less for deaths in 1984. The amount covered by the credit goes up each year until 1987:

1985—$400,000
1986—$500,000
1987—$600,000

There are six major ways to reduce your estate tax:

1. Lifetime gifts
2. Marital deduction gifts
3. $100,000 exemption for employee death benefits and individual retirement arrangements
4. Charitable gifts
5. Taking property you paid for out of joint tenancy
6. Paying the tax with bonds bought at a discount

Lifetime Gifts

Any gift, even if you make it on your deathbed, generally will get property out of your taxable estate, as long as you don't keep any strings on the gift. A gift of insurance on your life is an exception. If you make such a gift and die within three years, the policy proceeds will count as part of your estate.

Any part of a lifetime gift that is not covered by the $10,000 exclusion will still be counted in figuring your estate tax when you die, at the value when the gift was made. This is not the same as having the gift included in your taxable estate. In that case, it would be valued at the time of your death.

It is easy to see that any gift may save estate taxes to the extent it is covered by the $10,000 exclusion. But the part of the gift that is over $10,000 also may save estate taxes, for three reasons: First of all, the property you give may go up in value before you die. If you don't keep a string which makes your gift incomplete, only the value when you make the gift counts for the estate tax, not the value when you die. For example, if Louise gives Jennie land worth $100,000 and makes no other gifts that year, only the $90,000 above the $10,000 exclusion will count in figuring her estate tax, even if the land is worth $1 million by the time she dies.

Second, the income from the property after you make the gift will not be counted in figuring your estate tax. If you did not make the gift, any income you saved (after income taxes) would continue to increase your estate until you died.

Finally, if you have to pay a gift tax, the amount you pay will not count as part of your estate, if you live for three years after the gift is made. So you save estate tax on the amount you pay in gift tax.

Gifts do not always save estate taxes, though. The property you give may go down in value after the gift is made. And you lose the chance to earn interest for the rest of your life on any gift tax you pay.

Your lawyer can advise you as to whether in your case gifts are likely to save enough estate tax to be worth making for that reason.

Over the years, Congress has laid down rules as to the kinds of strings that make property count in figuring your estate tax, even though you gave it away during your lifetime. Three kinds of strings may do this:

1. Keeping the income from the property or the right to decide who gets it

2. Keeping the right to get back the principal
3. Keeping control over the principal

Let's see how these strings could enter into gifts Louise might make by means of a trust for her children.

Keeping the Income or the Right to Decide Who Gets It

It has been true for over fifty years that if you set up a trust and keep the income for your life, the value of the trust at your death will count in figuring your estate tax. What people sometimes do not realize is that even though the income is not payable to you personally, if it is to be used to pay your bills or support your legal dependents, the effect is the same. So if Louise has a legal obligation to support a child and the trust is to be used for that purpose, the trust property would be included in Louise's taxable estate.

The same situation may come up informally, for example, if Louise gives her child her house and then continues to live in the house. If Louise and her child had an understanding that she could do this, she has kept the kind of string that requires the house to be included in her taxable estate.

Keeping the Right to Get Back the Principal

If Louise sets up a trust for her daughter Jennie for life, then to go to her grandchildren, she may want to get back the principal if her child dies before she does. That kind of string would be likely to cause the value of the grandchildren's interests in the trust to be included in Louise's taxable estate, even if she died before Jennie and therefore didn't get the trust property back.

Keeping Control over the Principal

Louise may want to be trustee and to have the power to decide when Jennie gets the money. If she does (and the courts have been very strict in deciding when someone has kept this kind of string), the property will be included in her taxable estate. What Louise should do is to name as trustee someone else, who she feels will handle the trust as she would.

Sometimes people have tried to avoid this rule by naming someone else as trustee but reserving the power to fire him or her and appoint a new trustee. This is very dangerous, however, as the Internal Revenue Service says that if you have such a power, even if you can't appoint yourself as trustee, you will be treated as if you had all the powers of the trustee. This is likely to mean that the trust property will be included in your taxable estate.

Marital Deduction Gifts

Generally, if you are married, the most important step you can take to reduce your estate taxes is to make marital deduction gifts to your husband. If your husband survives you, this usually means that your estate need not pay any federal estate tax, because there is no limit on the amount that can be taken as a marital deduction for gifts to your husband. You can leave him everything over the amount that is tax-free because of the special credit provided by law ($325,000 for deaths in 1984). In order for your estate to be subject to any federal estate tax in this situation, the estate and inheritance taxes payable to a state generally must be more than the amount that is covered by the special credit. In that case, the taxes paid to the state would reduce what your husband receives. This *rarely* happens.

You may not want to make any marital deduction gifts to your husband, or you may want to give him less than the amount required to keep your estate from being taxed. This can be either because you would prefer for your children or someone else to have the money, or because your husband already has a substantial amount and you don't want to add to his tax problems. Before you decide to cut out or cut down on his gift, however, you should think hard about the cost in estate taxes for your estate. You should also go over the various ways to use a trust to get the marital deduction without giving your husband complete control over the property.*

You can get the marital deduction by leaving your husband property directly, without using a trust. You will also get the marital deduction if you own property with him as joint tenants or tenants by the entirety and he survives you. In that case, half of the

---

*See chapter 12, pp. 198–200.

value of the joint property will be included in your taxable estate. That amount will also be treated as a marital deduction gift to your husband.

Generally he must survive you in order for you to get a marital deduction for gifts to him. But you can provide that he gets his gift anyway if it can't be proved whether you or he died first. This is to cover the case where the plane crashes with both of you in it, and for tax reasons you want the deduction even though he didn't live long enough to enjoy the gift.

$100,000 Exemption for Employee Death Benefits and Individual Retirement Arrangements

If you are entitled to a death benefit under a qualified plan for employees, there is a $100,000 exemption from estate tax if the benefit is payable to anyone other than your executor. Whoever receives it also must satisfy other requirements imposed by law. The exemption applies as well to death benefits under an individual retirement arrangement (IRA) that you set up or under an HR 10 (Keogh) plan. You are limited to a total exemption of $100,000 under all of these plans and arrangements.

Your lawyer can advise you how this exemption should be taken into account for your estate. Sometimes it makes better sense not to claim the exemption, because in order to get it your beneficiary may have to pay a higher income tax on the benefit when he or she collects it.

Charitable Gifts

An estate tax deduction is allowed for property you leave to a qualified charity. It saves taxes to make the gift while you are living, because by doing so you can get an income tax deduction. If you wait until you die to make the gift, you get no income tax deduction. Either way, there is no gift tax or estate tax on what passes to charity in one of the forms recognized by the tax law.

From a tax standpoint, a gift to a charitable split-interest trust offers special savings and allows you to combine benefits for your family with benefits to a charity.* Another way to achieve this combination is to give the charity an interest in your home or farm, after the death of one or more members of your family.

For example, you can give your house to your daughter for life, then to a charity. The charity will have what lawyers call a remainder interest and will be entitled to the house when your daughter dies. Your estate will be entitled to a charitable deduction for the value of the charity's interest, discounted for a period equal to your daughter's life expectancy under the tables of the Internal Revenue Service, which presently uses a 10 percent interest rate.

*See chapter 12, pp. 203–204.

Taking Property You Paid For out of Joint Names

If you bought property and put it in your name and anyone except your husband's as joint tenants, you may be caught in an estate tax trap. This is because the full value of the property will be counted in figuring your estate tax, even though the other owner had a half interest in it. For example, if you and your daughter bought a house but you put up all the money, if you die first, the entire value of the house will be included in your taxable estate. (If your daughter died first, no part of the value of the house would be included in her taxable estate, as long as you were able to prove you paid the entire cost of the house.)

You can avoid this trap by changing the way title to the house is held before you die. You can give your interest to your daughter, so that she owns the house, or you and she can change to a tenancy in common, so that there is no right of survivorship when one of you dies. If you give your interest to your daughter, you are making a gift of one-half the value of the house for purposes of the gift tax. If you change to a tenancy in common, so that each of you has a half interest, you are not making a gift, but only one-half the value will be included in your taxable estate when you die. If you do nothing and are the first to die, the entire value will be included.

This rule does not apply to property you and your husband own as joint tenants or tenants by the entirety. One-half will be included in the taxable estate of whoever dies first, no matter who paid for the property.

Paying the Estate Tax with Bonds Bought at a Discount

You can arrange to pay your estate tax at a discount by buying certain issues of United States Treasury bonds during your life. These bonds sell for less than par (100 cents on the dollar) but can be redeemed at par to pay your estate tax. As this book goes to press, the discount is under 10 percent because none of the bonds that can be used for this purpose sell below 90. At times in the past they have been available for as little as 70.

The discount is not as big as it appears, because bonds that can be redeemed to pay your estate tax will be valued at 100 even though they are selling for 90. This means that if you buy $100,000 worth of bonds for $90,000, and they can be redeemed to pay your estate tax, you will have increased the size of your estate (and the tax) because the bonds will be valued for $10,000 more than you paid for them.

The bonds must be bought before your death in order to be eligible to be redeemed at par to pay the estate tax. Your executor cannot buy them for this purpose.

These bonds pay low interest rates—only 3 percent for one issue—and are not good investments. So most people who buy them want to do so as short a time before they die as possible, to avoid having to transfer funds from a more profitable investment any earlier than is necessary.

In order not to have to arrange for the purchase themselves when they are in their final illness, some people provide for payment of their estate tax by a revocable trust and authorize the trustee to buy the bonds. The trustee then can act whenever it seems advisable to do so.

PART VI

HOW TO SAVE
TAXES FOR YOUR
FAMILY

WHY *does a son or daughter sometimes say to a parent "Please do not give me so much in your will"? It is often because the child knows that a full share of your estate could cost heavily in taxes. Yet these taxes could easily be avoided by other arrangements that would still give your child all he or she really wants.*

The key to saving taxes for your family is quite simple.

If you leave your child a share of your estate directly, you immediately create tax problems for him or her. From the moment your child receives the property, he or she will be taxed on any income it produces. If your child gives it away, he or she will have made a gift for purposes of the gift tax. If not, it will eventually be counted in figuring the tax on your child's estate.

Suppose instead of giving the property directly, you set up a trust for your child. Then, instead of giving the full package of rights—and taxes—that go with ownership, you can pick and choose.

For example, you and your daughter may agree that her needs would be met by the income from a share of your estate, without the principal. In that case, it makes no sense to give the share directly, because that could mean she would eventually wind up paying gift or estate taxes on principal that wasn't needed in the first place.

You may be surprised to find how much control over principal you can give your child without making him or her pay gift or estate taxes when it passes on. The new generation-skipping transfer tax is intended to limit these tax-saving opportunities, but often there are ways to avoid it as well. Chapter 16 shows how you can save on all three of these taxes—gift, estate, and generation-skipping transfer taxes—and often still give your child a large amount of control over your property.

Your child may be more worried about income taxes than about taxes that won't be paid until your property passes on from him or her to your grandchildren. After all, income taxes must be paid every year. In that case, you may not want to give your child all of the income from his or her share of your estate. Again, there are attractive alternative arrangements that should provide as much income as is needed without making your child taxable on anything more. The rest of the income from your child's share can be accumulated in a trust until it is needed. It might, for example, eventually be used to put your grandchildren through college. Then it can be paid to them without having been taxed at your child's high income tax rates. Chapter 17 shows how to save on income taxes for your beneficiaries.

CHAPTER 16

How to Save Estate, Gift, and Generation-Skipping Transfer Taxes for Your Family

WHY SHOULD you worry about your child's estate and gift taxes in the first place? After all, if your child lives until 1987, he or she can either give away or leave $600,000 free of tax. It may look now as if that will be more than enough to cover all the property your child will ever own. However, there are two reasons you should be concerned: inflation and tax increases.

As this book goes to press, inflation has been

curbed temporarily and estate and gift tax reduction is the order of the day. But if you go back over the last fifty years—and your children may have at least that much time to look forward to—the long-range trend of both prices and estate and gift taxes has been generally upward.

Of course, things may be different from now on. You may be willing to assume that inflation is over for good and that estate and gift tax rates will not go up again the way they did between 1932 and 1943. But are you prepared to gamble *your* family's financial future on that chance?

If you want to save estate and gift taxes for your children, you should also take into account the new generation-skipping transfer tax. That tax is designed mainly to keep people from using trusts to avoid estate and gift taxes when property passes from their children to their grandchildren. The generation-skipping transfer tax came into the law in 1976. It is complicated and has been extremely unpopular with lawyers. There is a strong movement to either repeal it or simplify it.

The first part of this chapter discusses ways to save estate and gift taxes. The second part describes ways to avoid the generation-skipping transfer tax as it now stands.

Saving Estate and Gift Taxes

It is easy to save estate and gift taxes for your children because these taxes generally apply only to property one owns or over which one has what lawyers call a general power of appointment. A person holds a general power of appointment if he or she has the right to take principal either for himself or herself (or to pay bills) while living or for his or her estate (or its creditors) at death. In contrast, the right to dispose of principal by giving it to others but not to oneself, one's estate, or the creditors of either, is only a special, or limited, power of appointment. Federal estate and gift taxes generally do not apply to the holder of such a power.

The rules for life insurance are stricter than for powers of appointment over other kinds of property. Insurance on a person's life is counted in figuring his or her estate tax if the person has *any* "incident of ownership" over the policy. A power to name the beneficiary, to borrow on the policy, or to surrender it for cash, is an incident of ownership.

To save estate and gift taxes for your child, you should:

1. Avoid giving your child more money than he or she needs
2. Avoid giving your child a general power of appointment
3. Avoid giving your child an incident of ownership over insurance on his or her life.

Avoid Giving Your Child More Money Than He or She Needs

Suppose you want to give your daughter $250,000. You can do it in either of two ways—the high-tax way for her or the low-tax. The high-tax way is simply to give her the money. She will have to pay income taxes on the income she earns on it. If she gives it away, she may have to pay a gift tax. And if she keeps it until she dies, it will be included in her taxable estate.

The low-tax way can give her *almost* as much control over the $250,000, but without making her pay estate and gift taxes. All you need to do is to give her the money in trust, instead of directly. She can have as many of the following rights as you want to give her, without estate and gift taxes to worry about:

1. She usually can be the sole trustee, depending on state law.
2. She can have income for her life.
3. She can have the right to withdraw as much principal as she needs for her support in health and reasonable comfort.
4. She can have the right, in addition, to withdraw $5,000 or 5 percent of the principal each year, whichever is more.
5. She can have the right to leave the principal to anyone she chooses when she dies, except her estate or her creditors.

The reason you can give her all these rights without estate and gift taxes for her to worry about is that only item (4) is considered to be a general power of appointment. A special exemption covers item (4), except for whatever she could withdraw at the moment of her death. That cannot be more than $5,000 or 5 percent of the trust property to be counted in figuring her estate tax, depending on whether she has withdrawn anything earlier in the year she dies.

Your lawyer can include a provision to reduce the chance that even that small part of the trust will have to be counted.

Of course you don't have to give her the complete package of powers. This list merely is to show that you can go very far in putting her in the driver's seat for the trust if you want to.

Avoid Giving Your Child a General Power of Appointment

All this means is that if you give your daughter the power to leave the trust property to anyone she chooses when she dies, you must exclude her estate (and creditors of her estate). You can also give her another power not on the preceding list—the power to make gifts of trust property to other people during her life. If she does make such gifts, they will count for gift tax purposes, because she is giving someone else part of the fund from which she gets income and can take principal herself. But she may like having the power to make gifts to her children (or others) without waiting until she dies.

Avoid Giving Your Child Incidents of Ownership Over Life Insurance

Because of this stricter rule for insurance, if you give your daughter the power to leave the trust property to anyone when she dies or to make gifts of it to other people during her life, you should provide that these powers do not apply to any insurance on her life that is owned by the trust. It is as simple as that.

Avoiding Generation-Skipping Transfer Taxes

Although the generation-skipping transfer tax (GST) is mainly designed to keep people from using trusts to avoid estate and gift taxes, it also is easy to avoid, entirely legally, of course. The GST tax applies chiefly to trusts that people set up for two or more generations of their descendants. For example, if you set up a trust to benefit your daughter for life, then to benefit her children, the GST tax applies when your daughter dies and the property passes from her to her children. In this case, the GST tax is figured by adding the value of the trust property to other property that is counted in figuring your daughter's estate tax. However, there is a $250,000 exemption for property that passes from her to her children in the form required by the tax law.

There are five major ways to avoid the GST tax:

1. Use the $250,000 grandchild's exclusion.
2. Use separate trusts for each generation.
3. Use a single trust for children and grandchildren, but authorize the trustee to make tax-free distributions to the grandchildren out of income.
4. Give your children only a future interest or future power over the grandchildren's trust.
5. Give any powers over the trust property to an independent trustee.

Use the $250,000 Grandchild's Exclusion

This allows $250,000 to pass from each of your children to his or her children, free of GST tax, if it is

249

in the form required by the tax law. For example, if you have four children and $1 million to leave, you can give each child a $250,000 trust. When the child dies, if the trust property passes to his or her children in the right way, it will be exempt from GST tax except to the extent it may have grown beyond $250,000.

Use Separate Trusts for Each Generation

You may have $500,000 to leave to your daughter. If you give it all to her in trust for her life, there will be GST tax on the excess over $250,000 when it passes from her to her children on her death. If instead you split the $500,000 into two trusts, one for her and one for your grandchildren, the grandchildren's trust will not be subject to GST tax when your daughter dies. Hers will be, but can qualify for the $250,000 exclusion. Only the excess over that amount will be taxed, if the grandchildren get the money from her trust in the form required by the tax law.

Use a Single Trust but Let the Trustee Make Distributions to the Grandchildren out of Income

Distributions of current trust income are not subject to the GST tax. Distributions of principal to members of a younger generation (if the trust is for people in two generations) are taxable unless the grandchild's exclusion applies. However, you may set up a trust for your children and grandchildren and give a properly selected trustee the power to distribute income and principal to any member of the entire group. If the trustee makes distributions to both children and grandchildren in the same year, the children will be treated as getting income before the grandchildren get any. If the total paid out exceeds the income, the grandchildren will be treated as getting principal, and tax may be due.

If the trustee makes distributions only to grandchildren in a given year, the distributions will be treated as coming out of the current income of the trust for that year and will not be subject to GST tax if they do not exceed that income. Principal can be distributed to the children in another year, when no distributions are being made to grandchildren.

This arrangement, which is sometimes called an "AC-DC" trust, works only if distributions to different generations are made in different years. Otherwise, the children will be treated as having gotten the current income and the grandchildren the principal, and the income exemption will not apply.

Give Your Child Only a Future Interest or a Future Power

Your daughter may believe she does not need income or principal of a trust. She may therefore want you to skip her and have only her children receive money from the trust. However, at some point in the future she may in fact need money from the trust.

You may save GST tax by giving your daughter only what lawyers call a "future interest." For example, you may provide that she gets the income only after she reaches seventy or is totally disabled for a year or more. If she dies under seventy without having become disabled, there will be no GST tax on her death because her interest was only a future interest.

Be Sure That Any Discretionary Powers Are Not Subject to GST Tax

Suppose a trustee (or anyone else) in a younger generation has a power to choose who to pay money or property to, or how much. When that power ends, for example, on the trustee's death, there may be a transfer subject to GST tax. This can be avoided if either the trustee is "independent" under a very strict definition, or the trustee's power is limited to paying money to lineal descendants of the grantor who are in a younger generation than the trustee. If the trustee's power is so limited, it does not matter that he or she is not "independent."

CHAPTER 17

How to Save Income Taxes for Your Family

WHY WORRY about your children's income taxes? A married couple needs income over $60,000 to get into a 42 percent federal income tax bracket, a single person income over $41,500 to get into that bracket. And these rates only apply to part of one's income. The part that is below these amounts is taxed at lower rates, starting at 11 percent and going up as one's income increases.

Even in a high-tax state like New York, the top state rate is never more than 14 percent, and you deduct what you pay the state in figuring your federal taxable income. So the combination of the two taxes doesn't cost as much as it may seem to.

On the other hand, if your child is already paying tax at rates like these, do you really want to pile more on top, making him or her pay at even higher rates? Often the same income could do your child just as much good if it were handled another way.

Suppose you asked your daughter what she would do with the income from her share of your estate. She might tell you that she would spend part, save part, and give part to her children. If you give her the choice, she will pay income taxes on all of the income from her share at her top rates. If you give the choice to someone else, you may be able to cut in half the taxes on the part of the income that she would save or give to her children.

What makes this possible is the fact that income that is taxable to your estate, to a trust you set up, or to one of your grandchildren is often taxed in a lower bracket than income that is taxable to your child. The arrangement you set up in your will, or in a trust you create during your life, can control who is going to be the taxpayer for the trust income.

You can even give the trustee the power to choose each year who will be the taxpayer for all or part of the income for that year. That type of trust is often called a "spray" trust because the trustee can treat the income like water coming out of a garden hose and point it toward whoever seems to be driest at the time.

Some years the trustee may conclude that none of the people you are providing for needs additional income and that it would be in their best interests to accumulate the income and add it to the principal of the trust. In effect, the trustee can be authorized to point the income hose toward the rain barrel until a dry spell comes when someone needs the money.

When the accumulated income is paid out, there may be an additional income tax under the "throwback" provisions of the tax law. These provisions are designed to block the use of trusts to accumulate income to save taxes. However, you may be able to avoid the throwback tax too.*

The five keys to saving income taxes for your family are:

1. Avoid giving your child or anyone else in a high income tax bracket the right to more income than he or she needs.
2. Give a trustee the power to spray (or accumulate) income.
3. Use a trust to "trap" income.
4. Use your estate to "trap" income.
5. Avoid the throwback tax.

Avoid Giving Anyone in a High Income Tax Bracket the Right to More Income Than He or She Needs

Suppose you want your daughter to have access to the income of a $250,000 trust fund. You can choose either a high-tax route or a low-tax route for her. The high-tax way is simply to give her the income. She will have to pay income taxes on it. If she gives someone else the income, she will be making a gift.

The low-tax way is to give a trustee other than your daughter the power to pay income and principal to her if she needs it. That way, the hose can be pointed in her direction when she can use the money without making her pay income taxes on money she wouldn't spend anyway. If the trustee is someone

*See p. 259.

who can be counted on to act with your daughter's interests in mind, she may be as well off as if she had the right to the income herself.

The trustee can also be given the power to pay principal to your daughter, or to make loans to her from the trust. The Internal Revenue Service sometimes tries to treat loans as payments of trust income in disguise. But if the loan provides adequate interest and security, this should not be a problem. And a loan from your trust may enable your daughter to make a down payment on a house or to meet some other immediate financial need, without having to pay an income tax on the money she receives from the trust.

Give a Trustee the Power to Spray (or Accumulate) Income

If given the power to spray or accumulate income, a trustee can decide from year to year who needs it. In a given year the trustee may decide that no one needs the income and that it should be accumulated and taxed to the trust. By choosing each year to whom to pay income, the trustee may keep it out of the hands of anyone in a high income tax bracket. Of course, the trustee must not have the power to spray income to himself or herself, or to use it to support his or her children.

Use a Trust to Trap Income for Tax Purposes

For income tax purposes, a trust is a separate taxpayer, generally treated like an individual, except that its exemption is lower and its tax rates are higher.

If the trust can accumulate income, its exemption is only $100; otherwise it is $300. Its tax rates start at 11 percent, like an individual's, but go up faster. For example, a trust hits the 18 percent bracket if it goes over $6,300. A single individual doesn't get to that bracket until his or her income is over $10,800.

Despite the lower exemption and higher rates, it often saves taxes to have income taxed to a trust, rather than a beneficiary. The trust will only be taxed on income that is accumulated, or "trapped," in the trust. So the trustee can be given the power to pay out income and thus to control how much income the trust will have to pay tax on. It gets a deduction for income that is paid out. The tax on that income is paid by the people who receive it.

If given the power to decide whether to accumulate income or pay it out, the trustee can choose to accumulate part, which will be taxed at a relatively low rate as income of the trust. The rest can be paid out.

When the trust's accumulated income is paid out in a later year, or when the trust ends, someone who receives the income may have to pay an additional "throwback" tax. The throwback tax generally is based on the difference between a tax at the recipient's rates and the tax the trust actually paid when the income was accumulated. If the throwback tax applies, it may cancel out all or part of the saving from having the trust pay the tax on the accumulated income in the first place. But you may manage to keep the person who receives the income from having to pay any throwback tax. The tax generally does not apply if the person was under twenty-one or unborn when the income was accumulated. And if the person is in a relatively low tax bracket, he or she won't owe any tax anyway.

Use Your Estate to Trap Income

For income tax purposes, after you die, your estate is a separate taxpayer, generally treated like an individual, except that its exemption is only $600 and its tax rates are higher. The rates, which are the same as for a trust, start at 11 percent and go up faster than an individual's.

It often saves taxes to trap income in an estate because the executor usually can control the amount of income that will be taxed to the estate. Like a trust, the estate gets a deduction for income that is paid out. The people who receive it pay the tax instead. So by paying out income, the executor often can allocate income for tax purposes between the estate and the people who share in it.

The important advantage an estate has over a trust is that once income has been trapped and taxed in the estate, it is not subject to any additional throwback tax when it is paid out in a later year.

Some people have tried to keep an estate going for a long time to take advantage of the income tax savings. However, the Internal Revenue Service will not recognize an estate as a separate taxpayer after a reasonable time to settle the estate has gone by. After that time, the income will be taxed to the people who are entitled to it, whether or not the executor actually pays it over to them.

Avoid the Throwback Tax

The throwback tax applies to income that is accumulated in a trust and then paid out in a later year. If the tax applies, it not only may cost money but also will make more complicated and expensive the work of the accountant who prepares tax returns for the trust and for whoever received the income.

One way to avoid throwback tax is for the trustee to pay the trust income out currently instead of accumulating it. Of course, this means giving up the potential tax advantage of trapping income in the trust.

The other important way to avoid the throwback tax is to distribute any accumulated income to people who were under twenty-one or unborn when the income was accumulated. The tax law exempts such distributions from throwback tax, unless the same person gets distributions of income accumulated in the same year by more than two trusts.

PART VII

HOW TO GET THE PROFESSIONAL HELP YOU NEED FOR YOUR PLAN

No BOOK *can be a substitute for a lawyer. To make and carry out your personal financial plan, you need a lawyer. Even if you are a lawyer yourself, you should have another lawyer review the legal documents you prepare to carry out your plan because it is particularly hard to be your own lawyer. I always have any legal document I prepare for myself or members of my family reviewed by another lawyer. Chapter 18 is about lawyers—how to find them and how to work with them.*

You may also need an accountant. If you dislike preparing tax returns as much as I do, you will be much better off turning the job over to someone else.

The first part of chapter 19 has some suggestions about accountants.

You will need an executor to settle your estate. If your plan includes use of a trust, you will also need a trustee. The second part of chapter 19 tells how to find the executor and trustee who are best for your purposes.

Finally, chapter 20 deals with when you need to review your personal financial plan. An annual financial physical clearly is called for. In addition, particular changes in your life may make an extra review desirable.

CHAPTER 18

How to Find and Work with a Lawyer

THIRTY-THREE YEARS AGO my father died. His will named my mother and me as coexecutors, and we needed a lawyer to settle his estate. At the time the Korean War was going on, and I was a GI in basic training. The army gave me a week's leave to go to the funeral and do whatever needed to be done about his estate.

Mother and I naturally went to the man who had been our lawyer for longer than I could remember, and who had handled my grandfather's estate eleven years earlier. It never occurred to us to ask what he would charge. Over the years his bills, including his fee for handling my grandfather's far more complicated estate, had been reasonable enough.

Six months later we found out. I still remember

the shock. The fee he proposed was a percentage of the estate way out of line with what he had charged when Grandfather died and with fees in other comparable estates on record in the local probate court. So we fired him and got another lawyer. Of course, we had to pay him for what he had done during the previous six months. But eventually we worked out a satisfactory compromise on that.

This story illustrates two rules:

RULE NO. 1: Find out what your lawyer will charge *before* he or she does the work, and whether the fee will be based on time spent or on a percentage of the amount involved. You also should ask how long it will take to settle the estate. You may want to inquire how soon your lawyer will be able to arrange to pay out part of the estate so that people who have shares in it will get some money to pay their expenses.

RULE NO. 2: If you do not have confidence in a lawyer's work or fees, you always have the right to fire the lawyer and hire someone else.

When we fired our lawyer, we faced the problem you, or someone in your family, may face: how to find a lawyer. We asked a businessman who we had known for many years and could count on for informed and disinterested advice. The lawyer he recommended did a satisfactory job in settling my father's estate and charged a reasonable fee. So, another rule in dealing with lawyers:

RULE NO. 3: The best way to find a lawyer is to get a

recommendation from someone whose judgment and motives you trust, and who has had experience in working with lawyers.

Like every other rule, this one requires further explanation. Experience working with lawyers on one kind of legal problem may be little help in choosing a lawyer for something wholly different. You would not go to a skin specialist for brain surgery. The fact that a lawyer is successful in the courtroom does not make that lawyer the best choice to plan your estate.

Suppose you are moving to a different part of the country. There may be no one there who you have enough confidence in to ask for a recommendation. What then?

Your present lawyer is a possible source, as he or she may have contacts with lawyers there. Your lawyer also may suggest that you stick with him or her and not get someone else.

Usually, this would not be a good idea from your standpoint. If you are moving, you should have a lawyer who practices in your new state and who therefore would probably know its written and unwritten laws and practices far better than a lawyer in your former state. When you die, your old lawyer usually will not be able to handle your estate if you have moved to another state, because he or she won't be a member of that state's bar, unless he can prove that your legal residence at the time of your death was your former state.

If you want to stick with your present lawyer and are willing to put substantially all of your property in a revocable trust with a trustee in your former state, this may work out. Even with this arrangement, however, you need a will that reflects the laws of your new state and should have a lawyer there draw it.

Your employer or your union may have a plan to provide prepaid legal services, on a basis similar to some forms of health insurance. In some areas there also are legal clinics which offer routine legal services for relatively low fees. You may find either of these sources satisfactory. However, since these sources of legal services are relatively new, you should check first with people who have used yours to find out if they were satisfied.

If no personal recommendation proves to be helpful, you will need to get lawyers' names in other ways. Two possible sources are the American College of Probate Counsel and your local bar association.

The American College of Probate Counsel is an organization of lawyers with experience in estates, trusts, and wills. You can receive a list of members in your area by writing to the College at 10964 West Pico Boulevard, Los Angeles, California, 90064.

Your local bar association can give you the names of the officers of its probate and trust law section, who also are likely to be specialists in these areas of law.

Another possibility is to ask the dean's office at a well-regarded law school for the names of some graduates in the area. Not every school may be willing to help you this way. But if one won't, you can always try another.

Having gotten the names of two or three lawyers, you should arrange a preliminary meeting with each one to find out if he or she suits you. It is important to get your questions answered. If you want a lawyer to plan your estate, you should find out about both the fees and the time framework involved before making a final choice. You should bring along enough information, such as answers to the checklist in chapter 1, so that the lawyer has some idea of the complexity of the job.

This leads me to a final rule.

RULE NO. 4: The more time you spend organizing information about your property and what you want to do with it *before* you see your lawyer, the less time your lawyer will have to spend (and charge you for).

Time is a lawyer's stock-in-trade. A billing rate of $75 an hour or more is by no means unusual. When you save time for your lawyer, you are likely to be saving money for yourself as well.

Your lawyer may ask you to fill out a questionnaire about your property and where you want it to go. This makes sense, because it is important for your lawyer to have lists of family members and of what you own (and whose name it is in) right from the start. This way your lawyer can see quickly which arrangements might work for your personal plan and which would not be suitable. Also, a questionnaire is something you can work on at home at your leisure.

If your lawyer doesn't give you a form to fill out, you can use the information from the checklist in chapter 1 to help you prepare your own description of what you want to do with your property.

267

CHAPTER 19

Finding Accountants, Executors, and Trustees to Help You

WHO MAY you need besides a lawyer to help you in making and carrying out your personal financial plan? You need an executor to settle your estate. If your plan includes a trust, you also need a trustee. Usually, for tax reasons you cannot be the sole trustee.* And if the trust is not set up to save taxes but to provide an arrangement for managing your property, you wouldn't be setting it up if you didn't want another person to take on the job. Of course if the trust continues after your death or is set up in your will, you need someone else as trustee.

Whether or not you set up a trust, if your tax returns are at all complicated I believe you need an

---

*See chapter 8, pp. 151–52.

accountant to prepare them. It usually will save time and money in the long run.

Accountants

It is usually easier to get a satisfactory recommendation of an accountant than of a lawyer, as a great many people deal with accountants at least once a year at tax time and have some sense of whether or not they are satisfied with the results. If no personal recommendation works out, you will need to get accountants' names in other ways. One possible source is the society of certified public accountants in your state. However, not all of the state societies provide a referral service.

Another possibility, as with lawyers, is through a well-regarded school in your area. However, accountants prepare for their profession in a variety of ways. So if you want a recommendation from a school, it is not as easy to identify which school to call.

If you have a large volume of accounting work to be done—for a business or for several trusts—you may want to interview two or three accountants before you make your choice.

Like lawyers, many accountants base their fees on the time spent, and the better organized your data is when you turn it over, the less time is likely to be required. Some banks that prepare income tax returns appear to base their charges on a percentage of income reported. But even if there is no direct connection between the fee charged and the time spent, it is desirable to have your data well organized to reduce the risk that errors will be made. Accountants often give you a form to organize your income tax information for them and to be sure that nothing has been overlooked.

Executors and Trustees

You need an executor to settle your estate, and, if your plan includes a trust, you also need a trustee. Since both are fiduciaries who are responsible for handling your money, many of the same factors are relevant for both, although the following discussion refers to trustees specifically.

Let's go back to Louise, who wanted a trust for her children, Mark and Jennie, and Jennie's children. What are the factors she should take into account in making her choice of trustee?

In choosing trustees, Louise's basic alternatives are individuals and banks or trust companies or other professionals. The trust may be so small that many banks will be unwilling to act as trustee, or if they do accept the trust, the minimum fee may be unduly large in relation to the value of the trust property.

Sometimes individuals may not be an alternative. Suppose, for example, that Louise wants to give the trustee the power to pay income or principal to her children and that there is no one else whom she trusts enough to name as trustee. Her children cannot be the only trustees, however, because they would be deciding how much to pay themselves, which would be costly from a tax standpoint.

In that situation, Louise's only alternative is to name a bank or other professional. The professional may be named as cotrustee with a child (or with both of them), as long as only the professional can decide what payments shall be made from the trust.

If there is an individual in whom Louise has full confidence who can be trustee without unfavorable tax consequences, I believe that Louise usually will be well advised to name him or her rather than a professional trustee. Such an individual is likely to take far more interest in the trust and in its beneficiaries than even the most conscientious bank trust officer, whose attention is usually divided among a great many trusts.

Although the individual may not have the investing and accounting skills that are needed to manage the trust, he or she can be authorized in the document setting up the trust to hire professionals to do specific jobs. In that way, if the individual trustee becomes dissatisfied with the trust's investment manager or accountant, he or she can simply hire someone else. If the trust is not large enough to have an investment manager, the trustee could even invest in shares of mutual funds and obtain management and accounting in that manner.*

Louise should anticipate the possibility that an individual named as trustee may die or wish to resign, and that a successor may be needed. If she has full

* See chapter 5, pp. 90–95.

confidence in her original choice of trustee, she may be happy to have the trustee name a successor.

If Louise does give the trustee power to name a successor, she should include a provision to deal with the possibility that none will be named, or that the trustee chosen will be unwilling to act. A back-up provision should always be included to allow someone in the family to name a trustee whenever none is serving. In this way, it will not be necessary to go to court to have a trustee appointed.

Louise may name two or more individuals as cotrustees, and in many situations this arrangement works well. Sometimes cotrustees complement each other, each bringing different skills and abilities to the administration of a trust. In other situations, one of them will be the active trustee, taking responsibility for the day-to-day routine affairs of the trust, but consulting the other on any major decisions. This may be the situation if Louise names Mark and Jennie as cotrustees but in fact expects one of them to do most of the work. The other child will have a sense of participation and involvement, and of having been equally trusted by Louise, if named as a cotrustee.

Naming two individuals as cotrustees is not satisfactory if they cannot work well together. The result may be a stalemate, in which it is difficult to get decisions made about trust investments. One trust with which I am familiar was in that kind of stalemate because the cotrustees were barely on speaking terms and had opposite points of view about managing a trust. One favored stocks and the other government bonds; one favored a rather informal approach in administering the trust and the other wanted to dot every *i* and cross every *t*. The result was that often nothing could be done, and the people who shared in the trust were worse off as a result.

If Louise does not choose to name a non-professional individual as trustee, her alternative in many parts of the country is a bank (or trust company). In some areas, there are professional individual trustees or law firms whose members act as trustee. Both banks and individuals vary greatly in their effectiveness as trustees, and Louise should make whatever investigation she can before she arrives at her choice. She should consider the following factors:

1. The reputation of the bank (or individual) in the community
2. The bank's long-term record as an investment manager
3. The fee schedule

Louise's impressions of trust officers that she knows personally are also important, but she should keep in mind that the particular individuals will not be around forever.

Reputation in the Community

A bank's reputation in the community is made up of a composite of factors which cannot be readily measured. Louise's lawyer might be a good source of advice in this respect. Some important factors are:

1. Attention to individual accounts—whether the number assigned to each trust officer is unduly large
2. Continuity of personnel—whether there is so much

turnover in the trust department that the people who
share in the trust will constantly find themselves
dealing with somebody new
3. Common sense in handling trusts—willingness to use
reasonable judgment in exercising the trustee's powers and in determining whether or not court instructions are needed

This last factor can be important. Some banks have
a reputation for such excessive caution that it is said
that an income beneficiary can't get a distribution of
principal unless he or she doesn't have enough money
to cover funeral expenses. Other banks seek court
instructions too often, at great expense to the trusts
they administer. Although situations do arise in
which the document setting up the trust is ambigu-
ous and such instructions are needed, they can be
minimized if the trustee gives the document a careful reading before agreeing to act as trustee and in-
sists on whatever changes are needed to clear up
any ambiguities in the document. Any conscientious
bank or professional individual will make a point of
doing this.

Record as Investment Manager

Often the best source of information as to a bank's
record in handling investments is the reports of its
common trust fund. This is particularly true if Louise
expects her trust to be invested in the common trust
fund. However, past records do not necessarily fore-
cast future performance. Most banks tend to have a
particular style in investing, which sometimes happens to be in tune with current market conditions
and other times not. Consistently good performance

over the years, however, is reassuring, and consistently poor performance suggests that Louise should look elsewhere.

The Fee Schedule

In many parts of the country, fees for trustees are set by statute or by generally followed custom in the community. Annual fees may range from ½ percent to as much as 1 percent or more of the value of the trust. A portion of the fee may be based on trust income and the balance on the value of the principal. An additional fee may be payable when principal is paid out or the trust ends. In other areas there are major variations among banks as to how fees are computed and what the minimum fee is. Banks usually insist on charging fees under their schedule in effect when the services are performed, so the present schedule, like the past investment record, is no guarantee of the future. But as with a poor investment record, a relatively high fee schedule as compared to other banks in the community suggests that Louise should look elsewhere for a trustee.

The fee schedule also should be taken into account if Louise wants to name an individual to serve as cotrustee with the bank. If the individual is a lawyer or other professional, the bank may be willing to share part of its regular fees with him or her. But if the co-trustee is a family member or friend, the bank ordinarily will not share its fee. It may even make an additional charge because of the extra time needed to consult the individual before making purchases or sales.

Sometimes banks are willing to reduce fees computed under their regular schedules if the amount appears to be excessive in the light of the particular situation. For example, if it is likely that the trust will end in a relatively short time, a full distribution fee may be too high. Sometimes it is possible to obtain a reduction in the minimum fee applicable to smaller trusts if Louise or members of her family also have larger trusts with the same bank.

CHAPTER 20

When to Review Your Plan

DOCTORS DISAGREE as to whether or not you need an annual physical examination, but there is no doubt in my mind that an annual financial examination is called for. So much can go on during a year that you may not realize how it can affect your personal financial plan. You should make a point, once a year, of updating the checklist in chapter 1 to see whether there has been enough of a change to ask your lawyer whether your plan should be revised.

In addition to your annual financial "physical," specific developments in your own life or the lives of other people may make a call to your lawyer advisable. The events I have in mind are:

1. You or someone who will share in your estate gets married or divorced.
2. You move to a different state.
3. You sell property that is specifically referred to in your will.
4. You start a business of your own.
5. Your employer changes the life insurance or pension plan for employees, or you change jobs and have these benefits provided by your new employer.
6. The value of your property changes substantially, or you become entitled to a share of an estate or trust.
7. You or someone who will share in your estate has a child.

This chapter refers to changing your will. If you use a revocable trust to dispose of your property, it also should be reviewed to see if any changes are needed in it.

Marriage or Divorce

Your own marriage or divorce is an obvious reason to have your lawyer review your personal financial plan. You may want to make provisions for your new spouse or to delete provisions for the former spouse. In some states, marriage revokes a will unless the will indicates that it is made in contemplation of the marriage. Also depending on the state, a divorce may have the effect of revoking provisions that were made in favor of the former spouse.

If someone named in your will marries, you may want to change the provision for that person. The change may be either to reduce the risk that your property will pass from that person to the new spouse or to provide for the new spouse. Like everything else in your will, this depends on you.

You Move to a Different State

There are enough differences in state laws that I would make it a flat rule to have a lawyer in your new state review your plan after you move. The lawyer may say it need not be changed because of the move. But there are different rules about executors and trustees in each state that often may indicate a new will is in order.

If you are married, it is particularly important to have your will reviewed if you move from a state that does not have community property to one that does or vice versa. The move may greatly affect your husband's share of your estate, as well as your share of his.

You Sell Property That Is Specifically Left to Someone in Your Will

If your will leaves your house or farm to someone and you sell the property, do you want to leave them the proceeds or whatever you buy with the money?

If you don't, their share will have been reduced or cut out altogether as a result of the sale.

You Start a Business of Your Own

There are so many possible effects on your personal financial plan from starting your own business that I will only try to highlight a few of them:

- Do you want to set up an HR 10 (Keogh) plan to provide benefits for yourself and your employees?
- Do you need additional insurance to cover debts of the business?
- Who do you want to leave the business to?
- Do you want to arrange for your interest in the business to be sold to a specific person after your death?

Your Employer Changes Your Life Insurance or Pension Plan or You Change Employers

If your employer changes the life insurance or pension plan provided for employees, your plan should be reviewed to see how the change affects it.

If you have new life insurance coverage provided by a new employer, you need to consider how the choice of beneficiaries fits into your plan. The same applies to employee benefits. You may also need to deal with benefits under your old employer's plan, which may be affected by your change of jobs.

The Value of Your Property Changes Substantially, or You Become an Estate or Trust Beneficiary

It is obvious that changes in the value of your property can affect your plan. What you may not be aware of is that the moment you become entitled to a share of an estate or trust set up by someone else, the value of the property you have to dispose of may change even though the money hasn't been paid over to you. For example, if your parent dies and you are entitled to a share of the estate, that share is yours to dispose of even if you die before the estate is settled. Sometimes it may make sense to take this factor into account in your will before your parent dies, by including alternative provisions to apply if he or she dies first. You may not want to be concerned about revising your will shortly afterward.

The Birth of a Child, to You or Someone Who Will Share in Your Estate

If you have a child but your will doesn't refer to children, in many states an omitted child can take his or her share just as if you had died without a will. But apart from that, if you either are or may become a parent at some time, your will should provide for any children of yours and also name guardians for them.

You might also want to revise your plan if one of the people who will share in your estate has a child. If you leave property to someone not closely related to you who dies before you do, leaving a child, the child may not get the property unless you say so specifically.

If you keep your plan up to date in the light of changes in your personal situation, you should enjoy greater peace of mind—one of the most important results of a good personal financial plan.

GLOSSARY

MANY of the terms defined in this glossary are not used in the book itself, because I have tried my best to avoid legal jargon. You may run into jargon elsewhere—perhaps even from your own lawyer—and turn here to find out what it means in nonlegal terms.

Account. A report of an executor, guardian, or trustee of items received and paid out, usually divided into separate categories for items of income and items of principal. State law may require that the account be filed in court for approval by a judge.

Accumulation trust. A trust that either requires or permits the trustee to accumulate all or part of the trust income instead of paying it all out to a beneficiary.

Administration. The legal process followed after someone dies to collect and dispose of his or her assets in accordance with the provisions of a will, if one exists, and state law. Because administration often is conducted under the supervision of the probate court, it frequently is referred to as "probate."

Administrator (feminine: *Administratrix*). The

court-appointed individual who is responsible for settling the estate of someone who has died if no executor is named in the will (or the person named is not legally qualified or declines to serve). State law specifies the order in which the spouse and close relatives are entitled, if otherwise qualified, to apply for appointment as administrator.

Alternate valuation. For estate tax purposes property may be valued either as of the date of death or, if the executor elects, on the alternate valuation date. That date generally is six months after the date of death. Property that the executor has sold or distributed before that date is valued as of the date of sale or distribution. The executor's election must apply to all property in the estate.

Annual exclusion. The amount, now $10,000, which you may give each year to as many people as you wish without the gift being counted for federal gift tax purposes, if your gifts are "present interests." If your husband consents to treat half of your gifts as having been made by him, the amount is doubled to $20,000.

Annuity. Payments for the life of the person who receives them, made monthly, quarterly, or annually, usually by an insurance company. A "private annuity" is paid by an individual, usually in exchange for property. A "joint and survivor" annuity is payable to two people—often husband and wife—and continues to be paid to the survivor after the death of one of them.

Basis. For income tax purposes, capital gain or loss from the sale of property is figured by comparing the selling price with the seller's basis. Generally, basis is what the seller paid for the property, but this amount is subject to adjustments both up and down. Amounts spent to improve a building increase its basis, and depreciation allowed for tax purposes reduces its basis.

Beneficiary. An individual who is entitled to receive money or property from an estate or trust, proceeds of life insurance, amounts payable under a plan for employees, or other similar benefits.

Bequest. The legal term for a gift of personal property by will.

Bond. The usual meaning is a legal paper given by a corporation or government to a creditor, promising to pay back a loan. In estate administration, "bond" refers to a written undertaking by an executor, administrator, guardian, or trustee to carry out his or her duties. If an insurance or bonding company undertakes to make good any losses from a failure to do so, it is a "surety bond."

By-pass trust. A trust set up in such a way as to by-pass estate taxes on the death of a beneficiary. The most common use is a trust set up by someone who has died for his or her spouse for life.

Charitable remainder trust. A trust set up to make periodic payments to individuals for their lives or for a period of years, after which the amount remaining goes to a charity. The payments may be either an annuity, based on the value of the property originally transferred to the trust, or unitrust amounts, based on the value of the trust, determined each year.

Clifford (short-term) trust. A trust that is set up in such fashion as to cause the income from the trust property to be taxed either to the beneficiaries or to the trust itself, and not to the person who set up the trust. The minimum period is ten years and one day or the life of the beneficiary, whichever ends first, after which the trust may provide for the return of the trust property to the person who set up the trust.

Codicil.   A legal paper, executed with the same formalities required for a will, that changes or adds to the terms of a will.

Common law state.   One of the forty-two states that do not treat property acquired by husbands and wives during marriage as community property.

Community property.   Most property acquired during marriage by husbands and wives who live in one of eight states: Arizona, California, Idaho, Louisiana, Nevada, New Mexico, Texas, and Washington. Property acquired by gift or from an estate is not included, unless it is later commingled with community property. Income from separate (non-community) property also is not included, except in Idaho, Louisiana, and Texas.

Corpus.   Principal of a trust.

Court trust.   A trust for which accounts are required to be filed in the probate court.

Crummey trust.   A trust that satisfies the requirements for the present interest exclusion for federal gift tax purposes by providing that the person the trust is set up for will have the power, during some period of time, to withdraw amounts transferred to the trust.

Custodianship.   An arrangement to hold property

for the benefit of a minor in accordance with state law in a manner that satisfies the requirements for the present interest exclusion for federal gift tax purposes.

Decedent. Someone who has died.

Deed. A formal legal document used to transfer ownership of property, usually real estate.

Devise. The legal term for a gift of real estate by will.

Disclaimer. A formal legal refusal to accept benefits under a will or trust.

Discretionary trust. A trust that gives the trustee the power to determine how much income or principal (or both) should be paid out or to whom it should be paid, or both kinds of powers. Often referred to as a "spray" or "sprinkling" trust.

Distributable net income. A technical tax term for the limit on the amount of income of a trust or estate that is taxable to the people who receive money or property from it.

Domicile. An individual's legal residence.

Donee. The recipient of a gift. The donee of a power of appointment is the person who is given the authority to choose who will receive the property covered by the power.

Donor. The person who makes a gift. The donor of a power of appointment is the person who creates the power.

Dower. An interest given by law to a widow in her husband's real estate. Generally, dower gives her an interest in one-third of the real estate for her life. It usually applies to all property owned during the marriage—even to property her husband transferred before he died, if the transfer was made without her consent. Today the share provided by law for a widow in her husband's estate if she gives up any rights under his will generally is more important than dower. To claim dower, the widow must elect to give up any rights under her husband's will or to the share of his estate provided by law.

Election against the will. The right given by law, in most states, to widows and widowers to choose to take a share provided by law in the estate of the deceased spouse instead of the share given by the terms of the will.

Estate trust. A little-used kind of trust that satisfies the legal requirements for the federal estate tax marital deduction. The trust income need not be paid to the spouse for whom the trust is set up, but the trust principal and any accumulated income must be paid to the spouse's estate when he or she dies.

Executor (feminine: *Executrix).* The individual or institution named in a will to be responsible for settling an estate.

Fiduciary. An individual or institution that is legally responsible for managing property for the benefit of others. Common examples are executors, guardians, and trustees.

Fiduciary income tax return. The tax return required for an estate or trust.

Fiscal year. A twelve-month period ending on the last day of any month other than December. Generally, a taxpayer may elect to use a fiscal year on the first income tax return he files. Otherwise, it is necessary to get the approval of the Internal Revenue Service in order to change to a fiscal year.

Five or five power. A non-cumulative ("use it or lose it") power given to someone to withdraw each year the greater of $5,000 or 5 percent of the value of the trust property.

Flower bonds. Certain bonds of the United States Treasury that usually may be bought at a discount but can be redeemed at full par value (100 cents on the dollar) for the purpose of paying the federal estate tax of someone who owned the bonds.

Funded trust. A trust created by an individual while alive to which he or she has transferred more than a nominal amount of property.

Generation-skipping transfer tax. A tax that applies to certain arrangements that give interests or powers to people in two or more generations younger than that of the person who created the interests. For example, a trust for your child for life, then for your grandchildren, is subject to the tax if the relevant exemption for transfers to grandchildren does not apply. The tax is intended to limit the use of such arrangements to avoid estate taxes on the death of your child.

Gift causa mortis. A gift made in anticipation of some immediate peril to the donor by delivering property to the donee, with the understanding that if the donor dies, the donee is entitled to keep the property involved. If the donor recovers, the donee must return the property.

Grantor. The person who creates a trust. Other words with similar meanings are settlor, trustor, and donor.

Gross estate. All property included in figuring the estate tax when an individual dies, before deductions allowed by law have been subtracted.

Guardianship. Administration of the property and custody of the person of a minor or incompetent adult under the supervision of the probate court. A guardian of the estate deals with the ward's property, and a guardian of the person has custody. Often the same person serves as both kinds of guardian.

Heir. Technically, a person who inherits real estate when someone dies without a will disposing of such property. Often used to refer to anyone receiving any kind of property after someone dies, whether under the will or by intestacy (under state laws applying when someone dies without a will). Nonlawyers often use the word "heirs" to mean children or descendants.

Holographic will. A will entirely in the handwriting of the person who made it. In those states which recognize it, no witnesses are required for such a will.

Homestead. An interest in the family home provided by state law for a surviving husband or wife, free from the claims of estate creditors. The amount of property included varies greatly from state to state.

HR 10 plan (also called *Keogh plan).* A retirement plan with a self-employed individual as a beneficiary.

Incidents of ownership. An estate tax term referring to the kinds of rights an individual may have over an insurance policy on his or her life which may cause it to be counted as part of his or her taxable estate. The term includes the right to borrow against the policy, to surrender it for cash, or to name the beneficiaries.

Individual retirement account (IRA). An account any employed person can set up to accumulate funds for his or her retirement. Deposits in the account are tax deductible up to specified limits, and the income earned by the account is not taxed until it is withdrawn.

Inheritance tax. A tax imposed by some states on the recipients of property owned by someone who has died, based on the size of each person's share. The other common kind of tax on the passing of property, an estate tax, is based on the total amount in the estate, without regard to who receives the property.

Insured. The person covered by a life insurance policy. On his death the company will pay the proceeds to the beneficiary.

Inter vivos. Latin for "between the living." Refers to gifts and trusts made by an individual during his life, as contrasted with gifts and trusts under his will.

Interest-free loan. A loan which does not require the borrower to pay interest to the lender, unless the loan is overdue. The kind of interest-free loan used in personal financial planning to save taxes is due on demand by the lender.

Intestacy. The legal rules followed to dispose of

property not covered by will when the owner dies, either because he or she left no valid will or his or her will did not cover all of the property.

Intestate.   A person who dies with no valid will.

Inventory.   A document prepared by the executor or administrator of an estate, listing the items owned by the estate, and usually giving their values as well.

IRA.   See *individual retirement account.*

Irrevocable trust.   If the person who created a trust has no right to take back the trust property, the trust is irrevocable.

Issue.   Lineal descendants, including children, grandchildren, great-grandchildren, great-great-grandchildren, etc.

Joint tenancy.   Co-ownership of property by two or more people which usually carries a right of survivorship, so that if one joint tenant dies, the other joint tenant or tenants automatically own his or her interest.

Keogh plan (also called *HR 10 plan*).   A retirement plan with a self-employed individual as a beneficiary.

Legacy.   A gift of property in a will. The term usually is used to refer to gifts of personal property but may include real estate as well.

Letters testamentary.   The official court document showing that an executor is authorized to act for a decedent's estate.

Life estate.   The right to possess property or to receive the income of a trust for the life of the owner of the life estate. Occasionally, the life estate is for the life of someone other than the owner.

Life tenant. The owner of a life estate.

Living trust. A trust set up during the life of the grantor. Usually the term refers to a trust that the grantor has the power to revoke.

Marital deduction. A deduction allowed for federal estate tax and federal gift tax purposes for property passing to a spouse in one of the forms specified by law.

Mutual fund. A corporation or trust organized to invest in securities of other corporations or governments.

Noncourt trust. A trust that is not subject to continuing supervision by a court.

Partial distribution. Payment of part of the money or property in the estate of someone who has died to a beneficiary before the estate is closed.

Partition. The division of property that is owned by two or more individuals as joint tenants, tenants in common, or tenants by the entirety. If a court proceeding is involved, the court usually orders the property to be sold at auction and the proceeds to be divided among the joint owners.

Pension and profit-sharing plans. Tax-sheltered retirement plans for employees.

Per capita. A division of property among two or more individuals, each receiving an equal share.

Per stirpes. A division of property on the basis of branches in the family tree. For example, if your son and daughter are dead and the son has one child living and the daughter has three children living, a per stirpes division would give one-half to the son's child and one-half to the daughter's children as a group, or one-sixth to each of them. Often a law that refers to "per stirpes" in dividing property when someone dies without a will also provides that in this situation each grandchild would receive one-fourth.

Personal property. Property other than real estate. It may be either tangible personal property, such as furniture or automobiles, or intangible personal property, such as securities.

Personal representative. The administrator or executor who settles an estate. A personal representative who is named in the will is an executor. If none is named in the will or whoever is named fails to act, an administrator is appointed by the court.

Pour-over will. A will that provides for adding property to a trust created during the life of the person making the will. Usually the trust is a revocable ("living") trust.

Power of appointment. The power to choose who will receive the property covered by the power, within any limits specified by the person who created it (the "donor"). If you have a "general" power, you may choose anyone, including yourself (if the power is exercisable during your life) or your estate (if the power is exercisable only by your will). If you have a "limited" or "special" power, you may choose only persons specified by the donor and may not choose yourself or your estate.

Power of appointment trust. A trust that qualifies for the federal estate tax or federal gift tax marital deduction by giving the grantor's spouse the income from the trust property for life and a general power of appointment.

Power of attorney. A document by which one person gives another the power to sign legal documents in his or her name.

Present interest. See *annual exclusion.*

Private annuity. If you sell property to someone and the buyer promises to pay you a specified amount annually or oftener for your life, the payments are a private annuity.

Probate. The process by which property is transferred from the name of someone who has died into the names of the people named in his or her will, or if there is no will, the heirs determined under state law, after creditors and taxes have been paid.

QTIP trust. A kind of trust that qualifies for the federal estate tax or gift tax marital deduction by giving the spouse income for life but no control over the principal.

Quasi-community property. Property acquired in other states during marriage by residents of some community property states that is treated for purposes of division, on divorce or death of a spouse, as if it were community property.

Real property. Real estate or land.

Remainder. The owner of a remainder is entitled to possession of property or to income or principal of a trust after one or more life estates have ended.

Remainderman. The owner of a remainder.

Residuary clause. The provision in a will which disposes of whatever is left in an estate after gifts of specific property or sums of money have been taken out and taxes, creditors, and administration expenses have been paid.

Revocable trust. A trust that gives the person who created it the right to revoke it and take back the trust property.

Right of survivorship. The right of a joint tenant or tenant by the entirety to hold the property free of the interest of a co-tenant who has died.

Rule against perpetuities. A rule that limits the time in the future that a property owner can control his or her property. In most states, the limit is twenty-one years after the death of the survivor of a group of people living when the trust or other arrangement was set up.

Separate property. Property of a married person in a community property state that is not treated as community property. Generally, property owned before marriage or acquired by gift or bequest during marriage, and, in some of the community property states, the income from such property. If separate property is commingled with community property, it may all be treated as community property.

Settlor. The person who creates a trust.

Spendthrift trust. A trust which provides that creditors cannot reach the interests of beneficiaries to satisfy debts.

Spray (or sprinkling) trust. A trust which provides that the trustee may determine to whom income or principal shall be paid. Often referred to as a discretionary trust.

Stepped-up basis. If you receive property from an estate, you use as your cost, in figuring your gain or loss when you sell it, the value when the person died (or on the alternate valuation date, if the executor used that date in the estate tax return). As values have gone up over the years, it is referred to as "stepped-up," although in a given instance basis may be "stepped-down" as well.

Tenancy by the entirety.   A special kind of joint tenancy ownership of property in some states, available only to married couples.

Tenancy in common.   Co-ownership of property without any right of survivorship. When one tenant in common dies, his interest passes under his will or goes to his heirs.

Testamentary capacity.   The degree of mental competence that is required to make a will.

Testamentary trust.   A trust created by will.

*Testator (*feminine: *Testatrix).*   Someone who makes a will.

Throwback rule.   The method used to compute the income tax due from a beneficiary who receives a distribution of accumulated income from a trust.

Totten trust.   A special kind of bank account under which the depositor has control of the money in the account until his or her death. The account then belongs to whomever the trust was set up for.

Trust.   An arrangement under which property is held and managed by one or more persons (or a bank or trust company) for the benefit of the people named in the document that sets up the trust.

Trustor.   The person who creates a trust.

Unfunded trust.   A living trust with only a nominal amount of property, such as $5 or $10, in it.

Unified credit.   A special credit provided by law which frees gifts and estates up to a certain amount from federal gift and estate taxes. For people who die or who make gifts in 1984, the amount is $325,000. It will increase each year to $600,000 after 1986. Lifetime gifts that apply against the credit are counted again in figuring the estate tax, so that only one credit is given.

Unified transfer tax.   The provisions of the tax law which count certain lifetime gifts in figuring estate tax.

Uniform gifts to minors act.   A law in most states allowing gifts of property to be made to a custodian, who holds the property for the minor until he or she reaches a specified age.

Widow's election will.   A will made by a married person in a community property state which requires his wife to choose between having her one-half share of the community property and letting his will dispose of her share as well as his. A wife may make a similar provision for her husband.

INDEX

Index

Index

Index

Index